Whitefish

A JOURNEY TO DISCOVER
THE GREATEST FISH OF THE GREAT LAKES

HISTORY, BIOLOGY, STORIES, FOOD & TRAVEL

Jeffrey K. Leestma

M·P·P
www.MissionPointPress.com

For Tracy,
who accompanied me on this little journey, as well as the big one.

Mission Point Press

Published by Mission Point Press
MissionPointPress.com

Softcover ISBN: 978-1-968761-29-5
LCCN: Available upon request

Printed in the United States of America

"To save something is to want something saved."

Contents

Introduction

THIS BOOK IS NOT INTENDED TO BE A SCIENTIFIC DOCUMENT. The factual information contained herein about the lake whitefish can be readily obtained from a variety of sources.

What this book is, however, is a celebration; a celebration of a great and noble food fish that has provided sustenance for a thousand years or more to inhabitants of North America. This book is also a celebration of those who harvest it, those who prepare it, and those who enjoy it.

As an underrated fish relative to its trout and salmon brethren, the lake whitefish deserves a little propping up and a hearty pat on its little, and sometimes not so little, humped back. That's what this book is about.

Economically speaking, the lake whitefish is king. It's the number one commercial fish in the region. Millions of pounds of lake whitefish are harvested and consumed annually around the Great Lakes. Gastronomically speaking, the lake whitefish is also king, favored by chefs for its mild flavor, versatility, medium-firm texture, and its almost universal appeal. Its taste is not at all "fishy," and it adapts well to almost every style of preparation. Whitefish is good for you, too, and is a good source of heart-healthy Omega fatty acids.

While not considered endangered overall, the lake whitefish still faces some formidable challenges in the Great Lakes. The lake whitefish, once plentiful and inexpensive, is no longer one of the more affordable items on the menu simply because of lower supply and high demand.

In some ways, parallels can be made to New England's embattled lobster industry. Biologists are working feverishly to save the Great Lakes whitefish, to bring populations back to what they once were.

French explorer Antoine de la Mothe Cadillac, who served as commander of Fort Michilimackinac from 1694 to 1699 and who is credited with founding the city of Detroit in 1701, couldn't have said it better when he wrote of the lake whitefish, "better fish cannot be eaten, and they are bathed and nourished in the purest water … the most delicate fish of the lake."

The lake whitefish is a food fish. As one fisherman told me, "This fish has one purpose on this earth, and that is to find its way to our plates." It's as true today for us as it was for Monsieur Cadillac more than three centuries ago.

This project was fun, certainly delicious, and eye-opening in so many ways. I met so many interesting people. And if I learned anything as I undertook this project, it is this: To save something is to want something saved. Too many people depend on whitefish surviving in the Great Lakes.

Anyone who has enjoyed lake whitefish, served simply smoked on a cracker or prepared in the most delicate French cuisine style, will agree that the lake whitefish is worth keeping around for at least another thousand years. Hopefully, in even the smallest way, this book will help do that.

Enjoy the journey!

Call Me Lake Whitefish

Not too thin, nor fat, just pleasingly plump,

With a silhouette that shows off my little back hump.

Mostly silver with olive and brown,

For centuries I've been the "fish-about-town."

I'm called humpback, gizzard fish, or Great Lakes main dish,

In Ojibwe-speak, the noble *adikameg* fish.

Lake whitefish is my most common-called name,

And my reputation is one of the highest acclaim.

I like to swim where it's deep and it's cool

With my friends along with me in a whitefishy school.

As a fish species we're amazingly auspicious,

And, I'm told, we taste truly delicious!

That's why, as a fish, I am really quite great,

And there's a very good chance I'll end up on your plate.

Whitefish Biology for the Non-Biology Major

BEFORE WE GET TOO FAR ALONG in the world of lake whitefish, it's probably a good idea to understand what kind of animal we're dealing with. Don't worry; there will not be a quiz at the end of this lesson. So, let's begin with the scientific classification of the lake whitefish:

Domain: *Eukaryota*
Kingdom: *Animalia*
Phylum: *Chordata*
Class: *Actinopterygii*
Order: *Salmoniformes*
Family: *Salmonidae*
Genus: *Coregonus*
Species: *C. clupeaformis*

Okay, that's a lot to take in, so let's make it easy. The phylum *Chordata* means that an animal has a backbone. Humans are also a part of the phylum *Chordata*, so that means that all of us have a little something in common with the lake whitefish, aside from the fact that we both tend to inhabit some of our favorite restaurants.

The class *Actinopterygii* is what makes it a fish, specifically a fish with fins.

The order and family, *Salmoniformes* and *Salmonidae*, put the whitefish squarely on the salmon and trout branch of the fish family tree. Let's face it, if you're a fish, and you run in the same circles as salmon and trout, that's a big boost to your social status. The genus *Coregonus* makes the whitefish a whitefish.

This is where it gets interesting. There are about seventy different species of whitefish in the world, including a few that are considered extinct. Whitefish can be found mainly in North America and northern Europe, even the Arctic, in both fresh and salt water.

In North America, the lake whitefish, or *C. clupeaformis*, can be found from Alaska and British Columbia all the way to Maine and New Brunswick and points in between. They live in all the Great Lakes. Another way to get a sense of where lake whitefish live is to understand where it is harvested and enjoyed in quantity, which means Illinois, Michigan, Minnesota, Ohio, Ontario, Quebec, and Wisconsin. By the way, the word *coregonus* apparently means "angle eye" in Greek and the word *clupeaformis* means "herring shaped" in Latin, but it's all Greek to me.

All *Coregonus* whitefish look somewhat similar, but there are some notable differences. The lake whitefish, *C. clupeaformis*, has an upper lip that protrudes over the bottom lip, as opposed to some other whitefish that have a protruding lower jaw. This protruding upper jaw feature comes in handy, as the lake whitefish is primarily a bottom feeder, and the vacuum cleaner-like jaw structure makes it a breeze to feed on snails, small clams, mussels, and insect larvae that reside on the lake bed.

Lake whitefish prefer a cold-water environment. They generally live in depths of between one hundred and three hundred feet but will move to shallower water in the spring and fall and at night to feed and spawn. Lake Superior is an ideal whitefish habitat because the water is deep, cold, and clean.

Lake whitefish generally weigh about four to seven pounds when harvested, but it is not uncommon to see whitefish weighing easily twice that. They commonly grow to a length of about twenty inches, but again, there have been fish caught that have exceeded that length by ten inches or more.

The largest lake whitefish on record is one that was caught in Lake Superior in 1918 and weighed more than forty-two pounds! If lake whitefish are lucky enough not to get caught or preyed upon, they can live to about twenty to thirty years of age.

Lake whitefish are social creatures and will swim in schools, a characteristic that commercial fishermen are certainly thankful for.

Lake whitefish spawn in the fall and early winter in shallow water and they lay their eggs usually on stones or gravel at a depth of six to twelve feet. A female and male whitefish will rise to the surface, perform a little fishy dance, and release the eggs and milt to the stones below, where they will fertilize. The following spring, the young whitefish hatch and the little larvae must survive on their own, with no parental fish to watch over them. It is believed that only about 13 percent of eggs survive to develop into larvae. That percentage is likely to continue to decline, not only because larvae are eaten by larger fish, but because of the lack of nutrients in the water caused by invasive mussel species.

As the fingerlings grow, they find one another to form schools, finding strength in numbers to help avoid predators. Swimming in schools, however, also makes it easier to harvest them for human consumption. And when it comes to natural predators, northern pike, lake trout, and the invasive sea lamprey are at the top of the list.

Initially, the little whitefish larvae will eat plankton, and this is where they face their first survival challenge. Zebra and quagga mussels now carpet much of the lake bed and consume the plankton and other nutrients that baby whitefish need.

But once whitefish reach three to four inches in length, they switch to feeding on bottom-dwelling critters like insect larvae, small mussels, clams, and snails, and they now have a fighting chance to grow to mature size. In the spring and early summer, they are treated to a multitude of mayflies (also known as shadflies or fishflies) as they hatch on the lake bed and rise to the surface.

If you are thinking that the lake whitefish hardly stands a chance, you would be wrong. We want the lake whitefish to survive. Fishing for whitefish in November is generally prohibited, because that is when spawning takes place.

Governments, universities, and tribal researchers are working together to "train" whitefish to spawn in rivers again, something that whitefish used to do before the rivers became polluted or clogged by logging and industrial waste a century or more ago.

As a food source, it's hard to beat the lake whitefish. Whitefish are low in calories, about one hundred calories for a four-ounce serving, and low in fat, about 1.5 grams. That same four-ounce serving packs a whopping twenty-two grams of protein. Plus, the lake whitefish is just so delicious!

So now you know most everything there is to know about lake whitefish biology.

Class dismissed!

The boat, *Max B*, at VanLandschoot & Sons, Munising, Mich.

The Fishers

FISHING COMMERCIALLY FOR LAKE WHITEFISH is not easy. It is challenging. Even on the best of days, it can be a challenge. And it is unpredictable. Yet, for those who depend on it for their livelihood, fishing can be very rewarding.

For most of us, though, little thought if any is given to how the whitefish fillet we enjoy so much got to our plate. Fortunately, the time and distance it takes for a whitefish to get from lake to plate is usually a pretty short journey.

And it all starts with the fishers, the fishermen and women who harvest, process, and deliver fish to restaurants, smokers, and retailers. We'll get to the people in a minute. Let's start with the equipment. The typical commercial whitefish boat, a trap net hauler, is about forty feet in length, give or take. The cockpit is situated almost at the bow, and behind the cockpit, for about two-thirds the length of the boat, all the way to the stern, is a flat platform, usually without rails, and only a few feet above the surface of the water.

This is in contrast to a gill net boat, sometimes called a chub or herring boat, which is typically fully enclosed, bow to stern, a bulbous-looking craft that looks more like a crude battleship than a fishing boat.

What's the difference between trap nets and gill nets? Simply put, a trap net is a three-dimensional net shaped like a giant funnel. The trap net is weighted at the bottom with floats at the top. Fish enter at the large open end and swim until they reach the "pot," a net structure at the end that holds the fish and prevents them from exiting.

A gill net is a two-dimensional structure—think of a very large tennis or volleyball net—also weighted at the bottom with floats at the top. Fish become entangled in the net by their gills. While gill nets are often more effective in catching large quantities of fish, the gill net also entraps fish that are not the targeted species.

Commercial fishing in the Great Lakes is highly regulated, especially for fisheries that have state-issued licenses. Without getting into too much detail, the regulations can vary by state or province and also between tribal and non-tribal fisheries. State-licensed fisheries are generally limited in where they can fish, and when. And how deep. They are also limited in how they are harvested, using trap nets only. They are limited by quotas. And they are often limited to catching only whitefish, so anything else they happen to catch, like lake trout, have to be thrown back. Tribal fishers face fewer restrictions due to negotiated treaties.

A typical day for a fisherman begins early, before the sun rises. A crew, consisting of a captain and generally two or three others, heads out to check their nets. On board are large bins and lots of crushed ice. The fishing season extends from spring to fall, so some of these mornings can be cold. And wet. And dangerous. The crew may head out daily if fishing is good, or every several days if the fishing is not as good. Trap nets keep the fish alive until they are harvested.

When the crew reaches the net, the pot end is hauled onto the platform of the boat, either by hand or by electric winch. This is why a boat with low or no side rails is advantageous.

Once the pot end of the trap net reaches the boat platform, fish are scooped out. Unwanted fish, as well as undersized whitefish, are thrown back into the water to live another day.

The crew has to move fast, so measuring is often done simply by holding it up to a piece of wood of the proper length. The "keepers," usually seventeen inches or longer, are thrown into bins, and ice is immediately shoveled into the bin.

Once the net is emptied, it is repaired if necessary and then reset into position. Then, it's off to the next net, and so on until all the nets are tended to. When the boat returns to the dock, usually around ten o'clock or so, the fish are quickly offloaded and taken to the processing room.

Often, the processing area is adjacent to the dock, but increasingly the processing is done a few miles inland. No matter. The fish are quickly transported within minutes, still in their ice-filled bins.

One of the things that impresses me most about commercial whitefish processing is how efficient it is. In virtually every fishery I visited, the fish processing area was compact, with a very small footprint, often no bigger than a standard two- or three-car garage. My preconceived notion of a huge fish processing "factory" simply isn't the case.

The first step in processing the fish is to remove the scales. In this regard, I believe every fishery I visited uses a mechanical fish scaling machine.

There exists a machine for virtually every step of the fish-cleaning process, from scaling to de-heading, to gutting, to filleting, to pin-boning. But no fishery I visited had them all. In fact, I discovered that much of the processing is still done by hand. Removing the scales is a time-consuming process, so if you had to pick just one machine, a scaler makes the most sense. Even the best fish cutter can scale a fish in less than 15 seconds, I would guess, but a machine can scale a fish in the blink of an eye. The fish is placed headfirst into one end of the machine and instantaneously gets shot out the opposite side, minus the scales. Only minimal hand scaling is required at this point.

Over the course of my visits, I saw people with amazing knife skills. In just an hour or two, a team can process two hundred, five hundred, and even one thousand pounds of whitefish, and be done and hosing down the room by noon.

From there, it's a race against time to get the whitefish to market as quickly as possible, either to restaurants and markets or to the refrigerated cases at the fishery.

Whitefish from the Great Lakes are shipped frozen to Detroit, Chicago, New York, the East Coast, and points in between.

But because many restaurants that serve whitefish are so close to the fisheries geographically, fish are shipped fresh on ice. As such, there's a very good chance that the whitefish you enjoy for dinner was swimming that same morning.

Some fisheries hold fish for customer pickup, while other fisheries deliver the whitefish to their customers—not just to provide a service, but to ensure the quality of the fish all the way to the restaurant's door.

Another thing I discovered about the whitefish industry is that it is most often generational. The industry consists mostly of family-run businesses handed down from one generation to the next. The fishing industry as we know it is about 120 years old; many fisheries are now into their fifth generation of ownership, a few even into the sixth.

Why is that? For starters, it's a business that is very difficult to enter. New commercial fishing licenses are scarce or nonexistent, not to mention the difficulty in finding suitable boats, nets, and equipment. And it's not an industry that produces millionaires. One fisherman told me, "We hardly make enough money to pay the interest on the boat!"

So, if it's such a difficult industry, why even do it? Because people love their whitefish. It's that simple. Even though the harvest is a fraction of what it used to be, people still eat millions of pounds of whitefish each year.

As long as the demand is there, there will be families willing to brave the elements and the regulations to bring whitefish to your table. As one old timer said, "If we don't do it, who will?"

He's right. There used to be thousands of fisheries across the Great Lakes. Now, there are just a few dozen.

The Classic Great Lakes
Whitefish Meal

THE LAKE WHITEFISH IS A VERSATILE FISH. White, mild, medium-firm, with a large flake, the lake whitefish can easily serve as a substitute for most any cod, halibut, grouper, haddock, pollock, flounder, or sole recipe. But the classic whitefish meal that can be found in countless restaurants in the Great Lakes region consists of basically four components, and is usually offered as a platter, a sandwich, or a "basket" with fries.

The classic Great Lakes whitefish meal, actually, is a not-too-distant cousin of the world-famous fish and chips: a few pieces of mild, breaded, flaky whitefish, delicately fried, and served with a generous portion of French fries ("chips").

The Fish

Lake whitefish preparation varies, and it can be broiled, grilled, baked, sautéed, blackened, breaded, or fried, and many restaurants will give the diner the option to choose the preparation of their liking. Personally, I usually opt for the traditional breaded and fried, because I like the satisfying crunch you get before reaching the flaky white flesh.

The Starch

The potato rules and can be offered mashed or baked, or piped around the fish, but most likely fried, as in French fries. For whitefish sandwiches, the starch also comes in the form of a bun, generally a basic hamburger bun or perhaps a sturdier brioche bun. Don't expect to find anything more exotic than that.

The Side

For dinners, it could be the "chef's vegetable of the day," but otherwise, the side is generally coleslaw.

The Condiments

Tartar sauce and lemon. For lake whitefish sandwiches, it's tartar sauce or mayo, lettuce, tomato, and perhaps a slice of onion. The beauty of the classic whitefish meal is its simplicity. Fish, simply prepared, and a couple of sides.

Even though this may be the most common formula however, it is by no means the only formula. On the contrary, there are seemingly countless ways to prepare lake whitefish, and this book endeavors to illustrate the versatility of whitefish and the variety of ways it can be enjoyed.

Bon appétit!

Whitefish Chowder

LIKE POTATO SALAD, no two whitefish chowder recipes are exactly the same.

And whitefish chowder recipes are generally kept under lock and key, so don't even ask for it. The best you can do is to take a bite and try to reverse-engineer it, to deconstruct the ingredients, which, of course, is virtually impossible.

I believe that if you want to judge the worth of a seafood restaurant, eat a bowl of its chowder. You see, if a restaurant's chef is willing to put the time and effort into making a really delicious bowl of chowder, then you just know the rest of the meal is going to be great.

While it may be true that no two chowders are alike, there seem to be some universal ingredients.

The first is the seafood protein, which in our case is lake whitefish.

In most all chowders you will consistently find potatoes, celery, onions, cream, and, often, bacon. Some chefs like to start out with a *roux* of butter and flour. Others don't. Diced carrots can be used, as well as a variety of herbs and spices. Some recipes call for an acid like sherry or wine.

To paraphrase the great Will Rogers, I never met a chowder I didn't like. Yes, some chowders are better than others, but I can't think of a chowder I wouldn't eat.

Even so, this is what makes a great whitefish chowder.

For starters, the bowl of chowder needs to arrive at your table piping hot. There is nothing quite as off-putting as a lukewarm bowl of soup. The minute the chowder is ladled into a bowl, the server needs to get it to you pronto.

A great whitefish chowder needs to be creamy. This is hard to define, but the chowder should be neither too thin and watery nor so thick that a spoon will stand up in it. I have eaten both kinds, and neither are enjoyable. If you get a bowl of chowder with just the right consistency, you'll know it.

Next, lose the oyster crackers. I'm not sure why people insist on putting oyster crackers, or crumbling saltines, into their chowder. For starters, crackers alter the aforementioned consistency, and they don't add any taste. It's a personal thing, and many people must do it because a tiny bag or two of crackers are inevitably delivered along with the chowder.

If I had to guess, the habit of putting crackers in soup is a holdover from the Great Depression, when crackers were used as an extender because meat and vegetables were in short supply—much like how chicory was added to ground coffee when coffee was rationed.

But my reason for going without crackers is this: If the chef had wanted crackers swimming in the chowder, then he or she would have put them there to begin with. I respect the confidence of a chef who delivers a delicious bowl of chowder to a customer, *sans* crackers, forcing customers to ask for them if that's truly what they want.

Finally, a great bowl of whitefish chowder must have great flavor. That goes without saying, right? Yet, I can't tell you how many times I've eaten bland chowder, a bowl of whiteness without great flavor.

Whitefish by itself doesn't impart a ton of flavor, nor do the potatoes, so it needs to be enhanced. Bacon, onion, herbs, spices, and clam juice are often used. Beyond that, it's really up to the chef to get creative.

Rest assured that if I see whitefish chowder on a menu, that's how I will begin my meal, and hopefully, it will be a prelude to a really great dining experience.

Sikrom

SIKROM IS THE SWEDISH WORD for whitefish eggs, or roe. For those of you who have eaten caviar, or have eaten salmon roe, say, at a sushi restaurant, you will have an idea of what whitefish roe tastes like.

But *sikrom* is different. The eggs are smaller and golden in color, as compared to the larger, ruby red salmon or trout roe. *Sikrom* may not be to everyone's liking. For some, it may be an acquired taste.

But if you already enjoy caviar, you will find *sikrom* to have a lighter, fresher taste than typical caviar, which has a "fishier" taste profile. *Sikrom* definitely has a whitefish flavor. And like most good caviar, there is a slight crunch, more of a snap really, when you bite into the roe and the juice and flavor explode on the palate.

So, what is the best way to enjoy *sikrom*? The easiest way is to simply spread it on a cracker or a toast point. This way, you can appreciate the true flavor of *sikrom*.

Sikrom works well atop hard-boiled or deviled eggs, on top of an omelet, or as a garnish with a scoop of egg salad. If you have access to quality restaurant carry-out or fresh market sushi, *sikrom* is an easy way to take it up a notch.

Sikrom can be lightly sprinkled on top of a seafood pasta. And for an incredibly easy, yet elegant *hors d'oeuvre*, prepare some tater tots, smash them slightly with the back of a spatula, add a little dollop of sour cream and some *sikrom*, and you have some delicious finger-food *latkes*.

You may be wondering why we would eat the roe of what could potentially grow to be a mature fish, but *sikrom* comes from fish that are already being processed for food, so this is a way to use even more of the fish without waste.

Smoking whitefish at Carlson's Fishery, Leland, Mich.

Smoked Lake Whitefish

SMOKED WHITEFISH IS THE *MANNA* OF THE GODS, a divine gift for us mere mortals. It's that good. Smoky, rich, unctuous, intoxicating, and addictive, smoking may just be the best way to prepare whitefish, only because many other fish species simply don't "smoke up" as well.

There are many fish-smoking establishments in northern Minnesota, Wisconsin, Michigan, and Ontario. There's an explanation for this.

For perhaps a thousand years, the Ojibwe (Chippewa) and Odawa (Ottawa) tribes smoked lake whitefish in the northern Great Lakes region. When French and English explorers arrived in the late 1600s, they, too, discovered the irresistible flavor of smoked whitefish. In fact, whitefish, and especially smoked whitefish, became a valuable trading commodity. And when Scandinavians from Finland, Norway, and Sweden arrived in northern Michigan, Wisconsin, and Minnesota in the late 1800s and early 1900s, they brought with them a long tradition of smoking fish, and the lake whitefish proved to be a perfect substitute for the more fatty herring and mackerel they were smoking in the motherland.

The basic recipe for smoked fish is simple: fresh whitefish, a salty brine, and wood smoke. Initially, smoking fish was a great way to preserve it. The brine, the heat, and the smoke all combine to kill bacteria and to delay the decomposing of the fish. These days, keeping the fish refrigerated is a must, and all smoked fish is clearly labeled with an expiration date.

Today, there are seemingly countless places to purchase smoked whitefish. In the Great Lakes region, smoked lake whitefish can readily be found in stores; in restaurants; by the roadside to appeal to tourists; in standalone shops; or attached to gas stations or gift shops, with smoking often done on-site. Served alone, or on crackers or bread, and perhaps with a bit of onion, capers, or dill, there is nothing better.

There are fishers and there are smokers. And then there are fishers who smoke their own fish. Finally, there are those who sell smoked fish but neither catch it nor smoke it.

Most people don't know that when they purchase smoked whitefish, they are eating a highly regulated product. That's right. You're not buying fish from someone who wakes up one morning and decides to get into the smoked fish business. I spoke with many whitefish smokers, and while there are differences, there are some rules they must all follow, mostly as it relates to smoking time and temperature as well as shelf life.

I found that some smokers were willing to share their techniques, yet others were reluctant, because they thought some things are key to their own smoking "recipe." You might think that all smoked whitefish is the same. They aren't, but here are the basics of lake whitefish smoking.

The Fish

Smoking fish requires that you start with fresh, wholesome fish that is not damaged or aged. Fortunately, because whitefish flesh deteriorates more rapidly than some other species, whitefish are kept on ice from the time they are pulled from the water, throughout the filleting process, and during any transit periods. Lake whitefish receive tender loving care from lake to plate, so you can be reasonably sure that the person smoking your fish is starting out with a great product.

The Brine

Smokers will begin the smoking process by bathing the fish in a saltwater brine. But even here, there are differences among smokers. The length of time of the brining process can vary, as can the amount of salt in the brine. Some will use a refrigerated brine just above freezing, say 38 degrees Fahrenheit. However, others will use a warmer brine for a shorter period of time, not to exceed 60 degrees Fahrenheit, so as not to begin to cook the fish. When the fish are removed from the brine, they are rinsed thoroughly with fresh water and dried.

The Wood

Most smokers, I discovered, use maple wood or sugar maple, but a few smokers I spoke with use apple wood exclusively and some will use a combination, often supplementing maple with apple or cherry wood. "We like to mix in some kind of fruitwood," says one smoker. Yet another smoker avoids fruitwood due to potential pesticide exposure. Still others use hardwood pellets for efficiency and consistency. Despite the differences, the resulting product is always delicious.

The Box

The smoking box is generally made of either steel or concrete blocks. Wooden boxes can be risky for obvious reasons. Does it matter? Well, it depends on who you talk to. But there does seem to be one point of agreement: An old, well-used, seasoned smoker is better than a new one.

If you look inside a well-seasoned smoker, the inside walls and ceiling are pitch black from years of use. The walls and ceiling look charred, and every time the box is used, the smoke and the fat from the fish are absorbed into the structure. If you were to fry up some chicken in a cast iron skillet, would you prefer to use a brand-new skillet or one that had been used and seasoned for decades? Therein lies your answer. A seasoned box, with all of those layers of smoke and fat, imparts a flavor to the fish that is, oh, so delicious.

Some smokers will "clean" their boxes by removing excess char, but they never clean it so far as to remove all of that smoky blackness.

Time and Temperature

How long should fish be smoked, and at what temperature? This is one aspect of smoking that can vary widely. Regulations generally say that, at a minimum, the internal temperature of the fish must be at least at 145 degrees Fahrenheit for at least thirty minutes. Scientifically speaking, the smoking process has to be hot enough to coagulate the proteins throughout the fish.

First, let's differentiate between direct hot smoking and cold smoking. Cold smoking is created by using an indirect heat source at a lower temperature. The resulting fish still has a raw-like texture, like lox. Hot smoking is what we see mainly around the Great Lakes and is really the only way to smoke lake whitefish.

When it comes to smoking, most smokers take the low and slow approach. Some build a fire first and then hang the fish or put them on racks. Others rack the fish first and then build the fire. Some smokers smoke at a constant temperature while others vary the temperature.

Some smoke for four hours, some for six, some for eight, some even longer. And all of the temperatures and times must be diligently recorded, either manually or digitally.

After the smoking is completed, the fish needs to slowly come down in temperature, and then refrigerated at 38 degrees Fahrenheit or colder. Then, it sits in a refrigerated case, patiently waiting for you to buy it and enjoy it.

The Whitefish Road

The Whitefish Road

A Culinary Lake Whitefish Tour of
Northern Wisconsin and Michigan

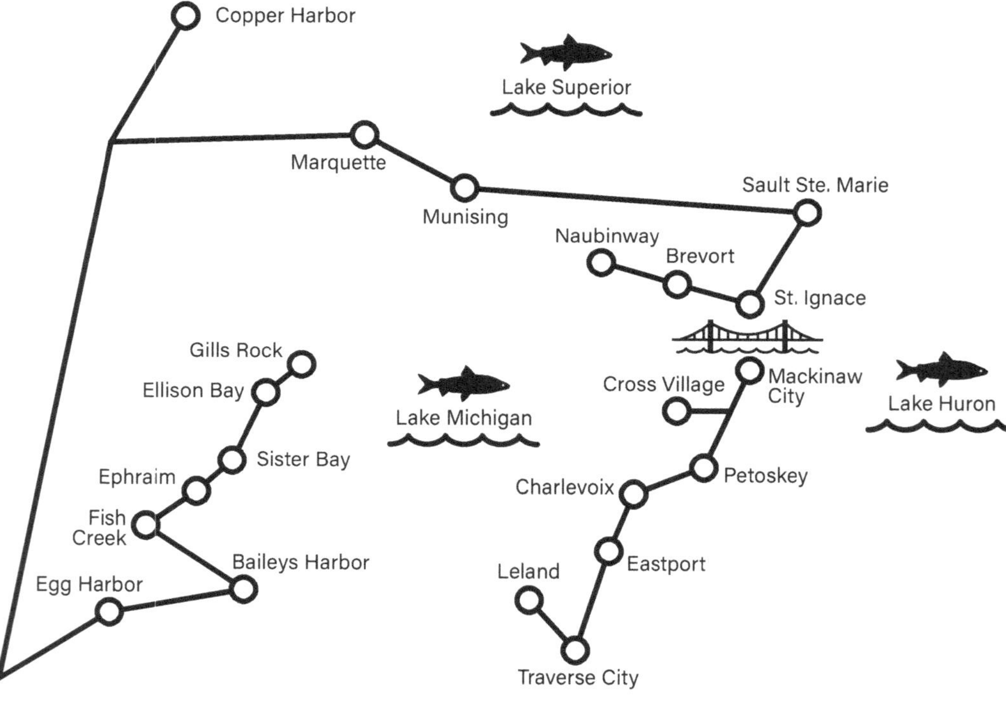

The Whitefish Road

WHEN I SET OUT TO WRITE THIS BOOK, I knew that I would be eating a lot of lake whitefish. I had no idea.

But the reality is that there are simply too many fisheries, smokers, restaurants, and shops to hit them all. Too many restaurants, so little time.

So, in the spirit of the Kentucky bourbon tours, or the Leelanau County or Door County winery tours, I've assembled a list of truly memorable places in Michigan and Wisconsin that prominently feature lake whitefish on their menus or retail offerings, or significantly add to the "whitefish culture."

And when it came to restaurants, I was looking for more than the traditional "fish and chips" approach to whitefish that we often see at diners, family-style restaurants, or by the roadside. Don't get me wrong. When done right, the traditional whitefish meal, served as a fillet entrée or in a sandwich, is dad-gum good eatin'! There are just too many restaurants preparing whitefish that way, and I would be stopping every several miles.

Since this book is a celebration of the lake whitefish, I was looking for restaurants that elevate whitefish preparations to new heights. It could be an entrée, of course, but also a chowder, an appetizer, salad, hors d'oeuvre, sandwich, whatever.

So, I've assembled some of my favorite places and compiled them into my "Whitefish Road." I actually traveled this road and visited the places I write about. As I said, there must be hundreds of restaurants that serve lake whitefish, but I simply couldn't visit them all, and to all those fisheries, smokers, and restaurants I couldn't visit, I sincerely apologize.

And I need to include a disclaimer of sorts. Like any restaurant menu item, things are subject to change. Some of the menu items I tried or wrote about may no longer be offered by the time this book is published. Also, please be aware that many restaurants are seasonal and closed during the winter months, so you will want to check before you visit. And, sadly, even restaurants come and go. It's the nature, unfortunately, of the restaurant business. But one thing is certain: There is no doubt in my mind that delicious lake whitefish will continue to be offered at innovative restaurants all across the Great Lakes region.

Our Journey Begins in Wisconsin

We'll start the Whitefish Road tour at the north end of Door County, Wisconsin, at Gills Rock. The **Shoreline Restaurant**, which as the name implies, is literally at the shore, with an incredible westward view of Green Bay. The Shoreline offers an irresistible appetizer of Whitefish Cakes with panko breadcrumbs, curry aioli, and spicy chili crunch. There is Whitefish Chowder, of course, as well as the signature Shoreline Whitefish, served hand breaded and fried, or blackened, or garlic-and-herb broiled, or baked with lemon-caper cream and served with a tangy remoulade or lemon caper tartar sauce. As I said, the view from the dining room is outstanding, and there is even an outdoor patio on which to sit and enjoy the magnificent sunsets.

Just to the south of the Shoreline Restaurant is **Charlie's Smokehouse**, literally a stone's throw away. Smoking fish is all they do, and honestly, when you do one thing and do it so well, customers will beat a path to your door. They do. I've eaten a lot of good smoked whitefish, and this is as good as it gets.

From Gills Rock, go south on Wisconsin Route 42 until you get to Ellison Bay. On the bay side of Route 42, you will find an authentic Italian restaurant, **Della Porta**. One whitefish item is offered on the dinner menu, *Pesce Al Cartoccio*, a whitefish fillet baked in parchment, with oregano, parsley, thyme, garlic, lemon, white wine, Sicilian capers, and roasted lemon, and served with potatoes and sauteed vegetables. It's not often that you find whitefish prepared in an Italian style, so this was a delight. For the daily brunch, Della Porta offers a Blackened Whitefish Burger with chipotle lime aioli, Cajun seasoning, and greens.

By the way, Della Porta is on the site of the now-gone **Viking Grill**, the restaurant credited with re-establishing the fish boil in Door County in the early 1960s. You can learn more about fish boils later in this book.

Down the road a bit and across the street you will find the **Mink River Basin** bar and grill, a big box of a building with five white pillars out front. Architecturally, it looks like a cross between modern Greek revival and a classic roadhouse. Inside, it's pretty much standard sports bar decor. Dark. Lots of TVs. It's the kind of a place where you will be sporting Green Bay Packers apparel during football season. Wear Detroit Lions, Chicago Bears, or Minnesota Vikings apparel into this place and you will get noticed for sure.

We chose the outdoor deck on the south side of the building. Mink River Basin offers the classic Door County Whitefish Sandwich, with grilled or deep-fried whitefish, lettuce, and tomato on a Kaiser bun, served with lemon and tartar sauce. For heartier appetites, order the Whitefish Basket, served with your choice of French fries or potato salad. You can upgrade to cheese curds. (Only in Wisconsin is whitefish paired with cheese curds. It works.) If you go home hungry from this place, it's your own fault!

But I ordered the very delicious Whitefish Reuben, with a large slab of deep-fried Door County whitefish, melted Swiss cheese, sauerkraut, and thousand island dressing on grilled rye. The whitefish held its own against the sauerkraut and the dressing, and I didn't miss the traditional corned beef at all. I still dream about this sandwich! A masterpiece!

Just south of Ellison Bay at the corner of Route 42 and Old Stage Road is **Henriksen's Fish House**. Henriksen's is first and foremost a fishery, and they catch all the whitefish they sell. Henriksen's supplies whitefish to many restaurants and smokers, particularly those on the west side of Door County. Once only a wholesaler to local restaurants, they have now branched out to creating and selling their own retail products, all made in-house.

In the refrigerated and freezer cases are fresh and frozen whitefish fillets, fresh and frozen cream cheese or goat cheese whitefish spread, fresh and frozen whitefish cakes, frozen whitefish caviar, whitefish chowder, whitefish soup, frozen whitefish burgers, and more.

They even make and sell whitefish treats for your canine and feline family members!

Further down Route 42 you will enter the village of Sister Bay. At the north end of the village is **Waterfront**, an upscale, dinner-only restaurant that really does food well, and if there is perhaps anything that can outshine the food, it's the sunsets over the marina. The menu changes frequently, I understand, but I was intrigued by their Panko Herb Crusted Whitefish, served with smashed roasted potatoes and a lemon caper sauce.

Further south, in the little marina district, there's a bright and airy place called **Boathouse on the Bay** that serves up broiled or blackened whitefish. Or you can do what I did: order a cold beer, a bowl of the Boathouse Famous Whitefish Chowder, and the Whitefish Po' Boy Sandwich. The chowder is creamy and delicious, and the fish in the po' boy is lightly battered and flaky and topped with lettuce, tomatoes, onions, and Cajun mayonnaise on a hoagie bun. Sit back and enjoy the beer, the whitefish, the boats in the marina, and, again, the incredible sunsets.

Continuing south in Sister Bay, we had to make a stop at the **Door County Creamery** for one reason only: their Smoked Whitefish *Chèvre*. *Chèvre*, of course, is cheese made from goat's milk. And the whitefish *chèvre* did not disappoint. It was a very tasty cheese spread, and the goat's milk lent a delightful tang. The Door County Creamery also sells gourmet sandwiches and gelato. The phrase "gourmet sandwiches" gets tossed around a lot these days, but these are true works of art. The chef-owners also own the aforementioned Waterfront eatery (as well as a herd of goats), and the high level of food carries through. Okay, I must confess, it was a warm day, and we ordered some gelato and took a walk down to the shore!

Right in the heart of the village of Sister Bay is a casually upscale fish and seafood restaurant called **Lure**. I think it's fair to say that you can't call yourself a fish restaurant in Door County and not offer lake whitefish, and Lure doesn't disappoint. Lure's offerings include Whitefish Almondine, with lemon citronette and toasted almonds, and Parmesan Crusted Whitefish, prepared with, of course, Parmesan cheese and lemon cream.

A Thursday special, at least at the time of this writing, is Whitefish & White Wine, local whitefish sourced from Henriksen's and available baked, blackened, or fried. And then, on Fridays, they have a weekly fish fry complete with cherry pie, a nod to the traditional fish boil.

The next stop on the Whitefish Road is the village of Ephraim, Wisconsin. The **Old Post Office** restaurant, which is connected to the Edgewater Resort, is famous for their nightly fish boils.

About halfway along the straight stretch of Route 42 from Ephraim down to Fish Creek is **Alexander's**, an upscale, fine-dining establishment known primarily as a steak and chop house, but they also offer chicken and fish. As for the latter, their Broiled Door County Whitefish is quite memorable, prepared with white wine, butter, and lemon. If you are looking for a traditional supper club kind of place with linen tablecloths and napkins and a beautiful décor, you'll be happy here.

And then, right next door, is **The English Inn**, an English pub-themed restaurant that offers the more standard broiled or blackened whitefish, but also the spectacular Pistachio Encrusted Whitefish served with lemon *beurre blanc* sauce, and the decadent Whitefish Oscar, which is baked and topped with bearnaise sauce, crab meat, and asparagus. The décor of The English Inn replicates a British pub but borders on a level of kitschy-ness that is both intentional and enjoyable. Your first clue is a metal knight-in-shining-armor sculpture at the entrance to the parking lot with a real flame emanating from its lance. Still, the food is top-notch, and the parking lot is always packed.

And in the adorably quaint village of Fish Creek, there is no shortage of whitefish dining options. At the upscale **LOFT**, every table is open-air, with a patio sunk slightly below sidewalk level, and an upstairs-loft dining area and bar. Because it is all in the open, the restaurant closes during the winter months.

I thoroughly enjoyed the LOFT's Whitefish Gnocchi of pan-seared, bite-sized whitefish, pearl scallops, mushrooms, tomatoes, herbs, and vegetables, served in a tomato cream sauce over made-from-scratch pillowy gnocchi. Their Baked Whitefish is topped with lemon Parmesan crust, oven-roasted and served over rice, one of the few times I've seen whitefish paired with rice. And a truly memorable plate is the Mediterranean-inspired Seafood Marinara, a combination of calamari and whitefish served with house-made marinara sauce over capellini pasta.

Also in Fish Creek, **Pelletier's** is well-known for its nightly fish boil dinners but also serves a very satisfying Lake Michigan Whitefish Plate for lunch consisting of a whitefish fillet with French fries, coleslaw, and served with Bavarian dark rye and tartar sauce. It's the perfect lunch for Fish Creek shoppers and sightseers. Like Pelletier's, the **White Gull Inn** is also well-known for its fish boil dinners, and one of the oldest establishments in Door County to do so.

From Fish Creek, we head east to Baileys Harbor on the Lake Michigan shore. Our first stop on this whitefish journey is **Harbor Fish Market & Grille**. The first thing you notice is how old the building is, constructed around 1908. Enter the front door and you are immediately standing in what used to be an old saloon, with the original wood floors, bar, and copper ceiling. The host was all-too eager to give us a little history lesson about the place, which was originally a Wild West-like establishment, including a few remaining bullet holes, and a little room off to the side where ladies, back in the day, would have to sit by themselves because they were not welcomed at the men-only bar. Thankfully, times have changed over the course of the last one hundred and twenty years, and today, Harbor Fish Market & Grille is an airy, casual, welcoming place where ladies and gentlemen alike can enjoy indoor and outdoor dining and a great view of Lake Michigan.

They offer Baked Whitefish served with rice, or Blackened Whitefish with Cajun seasoning and served with duchess potatoes. Make sure to try their signature Harbor Chowder which, for me, ranks among the best chowders I have ever eaten. We were there for lunch, and I ordered the Whitefish BLT, which features breaded and fried whitefish along with the B, the L, and the T on white toast. Instead of a fish boil, they offer a lobster boil, but we certainly won't hold that against them!

Dining at Harbor Fish Market & Grille was simply a delightful experience.

Great food, super friendly staff, and a free history lesson. They likely source their whitefish from nearby **Baileys Harbor Fish Co.**, which is convenient, because that is our next stop on the Whitefish Road.

Baileys Harbor Fish Co. is off the beaten path a little bit, down a long, wooded road that runs clockwise around the shore of Baileys Harbor. When you get there, you just know that this place is the real deal. Adjacent to the parking area is an old red asphalt-sided building with fishing nets wrapped on large spools, buoy markers, oars, and anchors nearby. There's even an old rusty fishing boat on dry land that has its glory days behind it.

The attractive retail market and processing building has been recently updated, and it has a welcoming hybrid Old West–New England look to it—a cross, if you will, between a Western saloon and an East Coast fishing shanty.

Inside, Baileys Harbor Fish Co. has every kind of whitefish product you can imagine, as well as flown-in fish from the Atlantic and the Gulf. For starters, they sell fresh, frozen, and smoked whitefish fillets and chunks. "Chunks" are pieces of fish cut crosswise rather than lengthwise. Fresh chunks are typically used for fish boils. And in the frozen case you will find things like whole cleaned whitefish, whitefish taco strips, whitefish chowder meat, whitefish burgers, and *sikrom* (whitefish caviar). Add to that frozen fish like yellow perch, walleye, lake trout, Atlantic salmon, Gulf shrimp, grouper, tuna, halibut, and scallops, and you literally have a one-stop shop for everything seafood.

From Baileys Harbor, the Whitefish Road takes us back to the Green Bay side of Door County to Egg Harbor, to visit **Mezzanine**. Mezzanine inhabits a chic, modern, pseudo industrial-looking building and no one embraces whitefish quite like Mezzanine. The delicious Whitefish Cakes are served for lunch and dinner and are served with Cajun-cherry aioli and fried capers. Mezzanine offers House-Smoked Whitefish Dip, Whitefish Chowder, a Whitefish Po' Boy, and Pan-Fried Whitefish. And on Fridays, all day Friday mind you, there is a fish fry that features two pieces of beer-battered whitefish, sourced from Baileys Harbor, and fries, coleslaw, tartar sauce, and rye bread.

We Travel North to Michigan's Upper Peninsula

From Egg Harbor we go south, loop around the bottom of Green Bay, past the city of Green Bay, and drive five hours due north to Copper Harbor, Michigan, where our next stop is the **Harbor Haus** restaurant.

You wouldn't necessarily know from looking at the outside, but inside, Harbor Haus is fine dining in classic supper-club style, with incredible views of Lake Superior. Harbor Haus is a seasonal restaurant, open early May through mid-October, and be advised that for much of the months of July and August and most summer weekends, Harbor Haus is booked solid. But don't let that discourage you. Give them a call for openings or cancellations, because they do whitefish right, and it's a most memorable dining experience.

Marquette, Michigan, is our next stop, where we find the **Vierling Restaurant & Marquette Harbor Brewery** housed in a building that was constructed as a "gentlemen's saloon" in 1883. The building has been faithfully restored and preserved. Upon entering, the first thing you notice is the long oak bar running along the left, exposed-brick wall. Wooden booths line the right wall. The original wood floors undulate just a bit, a testament to their authenticity. The Vierling is so close to Lake Superior that the whitefish could darn near jump from the lake into the frying pan! The fish is that fresh!

And with the availability of fresh whitefish, the Vierling doesn't disappoint. For starters, the Vierling offers Smoked Whitefish, a generous portion of flaked smoked whitefish, removed from the bone, served with crackers, dill toast, cream cheese, green apple slices, and a dill caper spread. I ordered Whitefish Bites, about a half-dozen oversized portions of breaded whitefish, fried golden brown. These are bigger than "bites," more like "two-bites," and they are served with the house-made tartar sauce. I could have made a meal of these!

I also tried the Vierling Whitefish Chowder, hands down one of the best I've had—rustic, creamy, with a hint of bacon.

For my entrée, I chose the Scampi Whitefish, a garlicky whitefish served with three shrimps and sautéed with red onion, pepper, white wine, and butter. Another entrée is the Whitefish Piccata, a grilled whitefish fillet served with a white wine, garlic, and caper sauce.

Or, you can order whitefish simply prepared, either grilled or Cajun-style. You can even order whitefish as an add-on to any dinner salad. I know what you're thinking, a few pieces of whitefish on top of a salad. No, you get a whole whitefish fillet, grilled or Cajun-style, gloriously draped across the salad, and a dressing of your choice.

We're not done yet. For lunch, the Vierling offers a Whitefish Sandwich served on a Kaiser roll with tomato, lettuce, and house-made tartar sauce, or served open faced on toasted French bread. They even serve Whitefish Fish & Chips!

Just a stone's throw around the corner, right at water's edge, is **Thill & Sons Fish House**. Brothers Adam and Dan Thill represent the third generation to run Thill & Sons. It was founded by Francis "FC" Thill in 1961 when he opened Thill's Fish House in the shadow of Marquette's historic downtown ore dock. The huge wood and steel dock still stands, albeit abandoned, and is a daily reminder of the history of the place.

FC's son Ted took over the business and now Adam co-owns it with older brother Dan, who captains the boat. And the business now includes a fourth generation learning the business from the water up.

While the Thills are licensed only to catch fresh whitefish, they make sure that their refrigerated cases are filled with a wide variety of seafood, from salmon, herring, trout, oysters, crab, scallops, even lobster. It is no doubt the one stop you make in Marquette if you want fresh seafood.

We leave Marquette and drive east forty miles or so to Munising, where we stop at **VanLandschoot & Sons**. In a recently updated retail store, the VanLandschoots sell a variety of fresh fish like trout, salmon, walleye, cod, and perch, but here, whitefish truly takes the lead role. In addition to selling the freshest whitefish from their retail store, they also sell whitefish and chips from a food truck in Marquette. Their smoked whitefish is smoked on-site, just steps away from the water.

We continue east across Michigan's Upper Peninsula until we reach Sault Ste. Marie, home to the Soo Locks and the waterway between Lake Superior and Lake Huron. Sault Ste. Marie is a big summer tourist destination, with people flocking to see the huge ore ships up close as they pass through the locks. Right across the street from the locks is the **Lockview Restaurant**. There are various places to eat in town, of course, but the Lockview is hard to miss with its iconic '50s-era neon sign. The Lockview is aptly named because large plate-glass windows provide unobstructed views of the steamships as they slowly rise and fall with the changing of the water level.

And if whitefish is what you are seeking, the Lockview is your best choice! The Lockview Restaurant is somewhat famously known for offering whitefish prepared six ways: broiled, pan fried, Cajun, deep-fried, lemon peppered, or Cajun deep-fried. And they serve whitefish for breakfast, lunch, and dinner.

For breakfast, they offer Whitefish & Eggs, which consists of two eggs prepared the way you like them and whitefish prepared in one of the six ways, with potatoes and toast. Also on the breakfast menu is The Poe, a toasted "everything" bagel with Smoked Whitefish Spread topped with capers and served with red onion and tomatoes. You can order the Whitefish Spread throughout the day as an appetizer, served with water crackers.

I visited the Lockview during the lunch hour, and I ordered the Whitefish Bites—perfectly deep-fried pieces of whitefish served with tartar sauce and a lemon wedge. With seven or eight big pieces of whitefish, there is easily enough for three or four people to share. I also ordered a cup of the Homemade Whitefish Chowder and the Whitefish Reuben, with whitefish battered and deep-fried and topped with coleslaw and Swiss cheese on rye. It was more food than I could eat, but I have no regrets. Every bite was delicious, and it's easy to see that all of the food is made fresh in the kitchen.

The Lockview serves a more basic Whitefish Sandwich, with lettuce and tomato on a toasted bun, and the Soo Locks Wrap … deep-fried whitefish served with lettuce, tomato, cheese, and tartar sauce on a sun-dried tomato tortilla.

Finally, the Lockview Restaurant offers traditional deep-fried "basket" meals of whitefish, or chicken, clams, shrimp, or walleye, all served with a hearty portion of French fries, with sweet potato fries as an option. And if that isn't enough baskets, the Lockview also offers a Whitefish Taco Basket: three deep-fried whitefish tacos in flour tortillas, served with coleslaw and a lemon wedge on the side. With fries, of course.

But wait! There's more! You can order the Lake Superior Whitefish Dinner, prepared in one of the six famous ways, served with two sides, the Fish Combo of deep-fried whitefish, walleye, and perch, or surf-and-turf style—whitefish paired with a center-cut sirloin. You can even get whitefish added to any salad.

Of course, the Lockview menu contains all the diner classics like burgers, hot turkey sandwiches, dinners, and more, all in a comfortable, friendly diner-like atmosphere. Come for the food. Come for the view. I recommend the Whitefish Bites!

From Sault Ste. Marie, we head south to St. Ignace. As we enter town from the north, on the west side of the main drag just before you get to the airport is **Massey Fish Co.** It's a little hard to find.

Turn west on Nelson Road and take it through a modest neighborhood until it ends. You'll see two large, gray-steel buildings. This is Massey Fish Co. and the tiny retail store is marked by a red door. They are mainly a wholesaler, and they use independent distributors who sell fish at about thirty farmer's markets throughout Michigan.

Massey is one of the bigger operations I visited. They catch and process all their own fish and provide it to restaurants and smokers throughout Michigan and the Midwest. They even supply fish to other fisheries that are limited in what they can harvest. In addition to fresh and smoked fish, they sell smoked whitefish *pâté* (which I very much enjoyed), whitefish livers, and whitefish caviar.

And while the processing operation is big, the retail store is, indeed, tiny, but you'll be able to find most anything you are looking for.

Drive south into St. Ignace, and you'll find **Manley's Fish Market**. You have to keep an eye out for it, because it is tucked back off the road, up a short gravel drive. Manley's has the kind of look that you would expect to find if you boarded a time machine and punched in the date "1955."

Manley's Fish Market was in fact founded in the early 1950s by Manley Pomeroy and not much has changed over the many decades. The shack still has its original tin siding, now painted in Green Bay Packer green with yellow trim. The current owner, who used to work for Mr. Pomeroy, is an unabashed Packers fan, and it shows. It's not unusual to see Packers fans in Michigan's Upper Peninsula, but generally on the west side of the U.P., where Lambeau Field is a just a few hours' drive away. Not so much on the east side of the peninsula, where Detroit Lions fans tend to dominate. But actually, as the crow flies, St. Ignace is closer to Green Bay than Detroit, so it shouldn't come as a big surprise.

Manley's is a fish market with a flea market vibe. By that I mean that you get the impression that stuff keeps getting added over the years, but nothing gets discarded. The walls are chock-full of vintage signs and paraphernalia. On the outside, Manley's could pass for a backwoods hunting cabin or canoe livery.

And that's precisely why you should visit Manley's. For the experience. And expect a matter-of-fact attitude from whomever may be working there. It's not that they are unfriendly, it's just that they aren't particularly chatty. But come for the on-site smoked whitefish, and especially the smoked whitefish dip, both of which are truly delicious and have earned a loyal following with tourists and locals alike. You won't be disappointed.

We continue south into St. Ignace, and we come to **Mackinac Grille & Patio Bar**. This place is right in town and on the water. It is open only during the summer months, and the vibe is decidedly Caribbean, particularly on the water side. It's a relaxed place with lots of outdoor dining spaces. It's also a very popular place and is often crowded, especially when a tour bus pulls into the parking lot. On the night we were there, there were many celebrating sailors who had participated in the annual Port Huron-to-Mackinac Race. As such, the waitstaff was stressed at times. But we were in no hurry. We had an outside table and enjoyed watching the ferries go back and forth between St. Ignace and Mackinac Island.

If you are in St. Ignace and you want whitefish, the Mackinac Grille gives you plenty of options. You can start out with the Smoked Whitefish Dip or the Mackinac Whitefish Cakes—flaked whitefish mixed with an herb stuffing and served with tartar sauce.

The Mackinac Whitefish Hoagie consists of a nice piece of deep-fried whitefish on a hoagie bun and served with lettuce, tomato, lemon, and tartar sauce. Also in the sandwich category is the Whitefish Patty Melt, which is a whitefish cake served on grilled rye with melted cheese and grilled onions.

The Whitefish Caesar is precisely what it sounds like, a classic Caesar salad topped with your choice of deep-fried or baked whitefish.

For entrées, the most popular dish is the Poorman's Whitefish, the recommendation of our server. This dish is whitefish brushed with butter and herbs and baked in foil with potatoes, broccoli, mushrooms, tomatoes, and onions. I'm not usually a fan of food cooked in foil, but we were sitting outdoors, and it worked. And it was delicious.

Mackinac Grille also offers a Brisket and Whitefish Combo—sliced smoked beef brisket and deep-fried whitefish. Finally, if you want whitefish prepared in the classic style, you can opt for the Great Lakes Whitefish—lightly breaded and deep-fried lake whitefish served with lemon, hush puppies, tartar or cocktail sauce, and, you guessed it, potatoes or slaw.

From St. Ignace, we take a detour west, to visit two places known for their smoked whitefish, **Country Smoked Fish** just a few miles out of town, and **Gustafson's**, further west in Brevort. Both smoke their whitefish on-site, and both are delicious. Gustafson's is the better-known place, but Country Smoked Fish is the more charming of the two. Both sell smoked fish as well as beef jerky and other items.

Heading South to Michigan's Northern Lower

Having loaded up on smoked whitefish, we cross the Mackinac Bridge into Michigan's Lower Peninsula and Mackinaw City.

You may be wondering why the area is spelled both Mackinac and Mackinaw. It's not a typo. Mackinac is the French spelling and Mackinaw is the English spelling of the Ojibwe (Chippewa) word "Michilimackinac," which means "place of the Great Turtle," referring to Mackinac Island and how it looks like a giant turtle rising up out of the water. It's pronounced "Mack-i-naw" regardless of how it is spelled.

There are plenty of places to get whitefish in Mackinaw City, and many of them serve whitefish in innovative ways, like **The Lighthouse Restaurant**, that offers Whitefish Almondine, Crab and Shrimp Stuffed Whitefish, Lemon Caper Whitefish, Macadamia Encrusted Whitefish, and Parmigiano Encrusted Whitefish. Or **The Hook Lakeside Grill** that features Whitefish Rangoons, a housemade blend of smoked whitefish and creamy cheeses wrapped in wonton shells and deep-fried.

But I stopped at **Audie's Restaurant** at the south end of the Mackinac Bridge because it is one of the longest continuously operated restaurants in Mackinaw City, and because they offer whitefish ten different ways!

We begin with breakfast and what Audie's calls the Fisherman's Catch, which consists of broiled whitefish, two eggs, and hash browns. It's still a rarity to find whitefish on breakfast menus, and Audie's doesn't disappoint. You can also add whitefish to any salad at Audie's.

Now, about those ten ways. Audie's offers whitefish Parmesan Encrusted (with breadcrumbs, herbs, and grated Parmesan), Broiled, Sautéed, Deep-Fried, Almondine (topped with slivered almonds), Planked (traditionally served on a maple board with duchess potatoes and a vegetable medley), Stuffed (topped with a decadent seafood dressing of shrimp, crab, clams, langostinos, and scallops), New Orleans-style, the spicier Cajun-style, and the super delicious Charlevoix Whitefish, a fillet dusted with Drake's, sautéed, then covered with house-made lemon-dill and caper hollandaise sauce.

In addition to those ten preparations, Audie's offers its version of the classic whitefish sandwich, the Whitefish Deluxe, with lettuce, tomato, and lemon dill tartar sauce on a Kaiser bun, served with French fries and coleslaw.

Before leaving Mackinaw City, we head about a mile southeast of town to **Big Stone Bay Fishery**. Big Stone Bay is a local favorite for Lake Huron-sourced whitefish as well as other locally sourced fish like smelt, salmon, trout, walleye, and perch. And they also "import" seafood from the East Coast, like herring, lobster, scallops, cod, and red snapper.

The day I stopped by I went to the front door and it was locked. I looked at my watch and it was a few minutes past three o'clock in the afternoon. I noticed the sign on the door that said Big Stone Bay closes daily at three (open later during the tourist season). As I turned to leave, I heard the door unlock.

"Hello!" said a man with a beard. "I was just about to flip the 'closed' sign in the window, and I saw you standing there. Come on in!" All the lights had already been turned off. "How can I help you?"

I selected a smoked whitefish fillet from the refrigerated case. The fillet came to seven dollars, and I handed him a ten. "Keep the change," I said.

"Are you sure?"

"Of course," I answered. "If you weren't kind enough to let me in, I'd be leaving empty handed!"

Heading south on U.S. 31, we take a detour at the town of Levering, Michigan, and head west to Cross Village, where we find **Legs Inn**. Legs Inn is open only in the summer, and it is a tourist hot spot. They don't take reservations, so don't be surprised if you have to wait, sometimes upwards of an hour or more. It's worth the wait.

Legs Inn is one of the most whimsical restaurants you will ever encounter. The structure is large-scale folk art, with sculptures, railings, and beams made of hand-carved logs, roots, and driftwood. Tables and chairs are carved out of tree trunks. The walls are log cabin-style, and there is shellacked wood everywhere: on the floor, walls, and ceilings. And on those walls you will find deer heads and assorted other stuffed animals, as well as wood carvings and tribal art and artifacts.

But the most notable feature of the stone-and-timber Legs Inn are the dozens of cast iron stove legs attached upside down on the roof as decoration. I tried counting the legs on the roof but gave up after reaching one hundred. This is the architectural feature, by the way, that gives the restaurant its unique name.

Legs Inn is the brainchild of the late Stanislav "Stanley" Smolak, a Polish immigrant who constructed the building in the 1920s with the help of his Odawa (Ottawa) and Ojibwe (Chippewa) neighbors. Stanley was also a self-taught woodcarver and artist and responsible for the fairy-tale décor.

Known primarily for its authentic Polish cuisine, Legs Inn also takes its whitefish very, very seriously. You can start with smoked whitefish or the house-prepared Smoked Whitefish Spread, both of which are served with crackers. Or better yet, opt for the refreshing Whitefish Avocado Toast: smoked whitefish and avocado on toasted rye, and topped with fresh cucumber, pickled red onion, radishes, and house dressing.

Prior to your entrée, you can enjoy the Waugoshance Salad, named after Michigan's Waugoshance Point (*waugoshance* is an Ojibwe/French word meaning "fox cove"). The Waugoshance Salad is a delightful combination of smoked whitefish, mixed greens, cucumbers, dried cranberries, and almonds, and tossed in house-made lemon sesame vinaigrette.

There is the popular Straits Whitefish Platter, a broiled whitefish fillet served on a ciabatta roll with lettuce, tomato, and tartar sauce. You can also get the Whitefish Platter in blackened form. If you prefer your whitefish not as a sandwich, you can order it as an entrée, again, either broiled or blackened.

And we're saving the best for last, the Legs Inn Whitefish Polonaise, a unique presentation of broiled whitefish, seasoned and served with sautéed mushrooms and onions, and topped with Parmesan cheese.

We head back east to U.S. 31 and continue south to Petoskey. Here we find the **Side Door Saloon** on the north end of town. While some of the restaurants featured on the Whitefish Road tend to be what I would consider "finer dining," the Side Door Saloon is decidedly, and proudly, casual. It's dark inside, with few windows, although there is an outdoor dining patio during the summer months. The walls are chock-full of antique and vintage signs and memorabilia. It's the kind of traditional place where the burgers are not grilled in the kitchen, they're grilled at the bar. Employees wear t-shirts with the slogan, "Everyone here brings happiness … some when they enter, some when they leave." Did I mention that this place is casual?

But I didn't come for the burgers, which are really good, by the way. I came for the whitefish. For starters, they offer a Greek salad, a Caesar salad, and a spinach salad, on which you can add smoked or blackened whitefish. There's a Lake Superior Whitefish Sandwich, served blackened on ciabatta bread, with tartar sauce, lettuce, and tomato. For dinner, the Side Door offers fresh whitefish three ways: blackened, with pistachio herb butter, or Grenoble, with lemon, tomato, and capers. And then there's my favorite, the Smoked Whitefish Quesadilla, with locally sourced Plath's smoked whitefish, herb cream cheese, cheddar-jack cheese, and *pico de gallo* served with seasoned sour cream. It's listed under the appetizer section of the menu, but it's more than enough for an entrée if you don't share. Which I didn't.

While in Petoskey, no visit is complete without a stop at the aforementioned **Plath's Famous Smoked Meats**. Smoked whitefish, admittedly, is a very small part of what they do, and it is not always available. It can usually be found in the refrigerated case on Thursdays and Fridays. But even if you don't see it, ask for it like I did. They might have some in the back.

I've visited many smokers on this journey, but Plath's is smoked-meat heaven. Yes, smoked fish, whitefish, and salmon, but also smoked pork (ham, chops, ribs, bacon, hocks), smoked chicken, smoked turkey, smoked lamb, smoked cheeses, and more smoked sausages than you can shake the proverbial stick at.

Plath's, still family owned and run, is worth the stop, either in Petoskey or at the flagship Rogers City location. The folks there are super friendly, and the smoked whitefish is what you would expect from people who know their way around a smokehouse.

We head into downtown Petoskey to a cute little lunch and brunch place, **Sam's Graces Café**. The day we visited was a warm and sunny September morning, so we opted to eat at one of the sidewalk bistro tables.

Sam's Graces has only one whitefish item on the menu, and it's only available for brunch: the Smoked Whitefish Benedict. This version of Eggs Benedict consists of a house-made English muffin (I mean, really, who makes their own English muffins?), a generous portion of flaky, smoky whitefish, two perfectly poached eggs, diced red onion, capers, red and yellow cherry tomatoes, all drenched in a rich hollandaise sauce, and topped with delicate young microgreens. With the reds, purples, yellows, and greens, it was a fiesta on a plate, and quite honestly, one of the best things I have ever eaten.

Any lake whitefish journey in Northern Michigan would not be complete without a stop at **John Cross Fish Market** in Charlevoix, on the south side of Round Lake. Round Lake is the little body of water between Lake Michigan and beautiful Lake Charlevoix. John Cross has been a Charlevoix institution for a very long time.

Long before the big summer homes and the expensive condos and boat slips that now dot the shore of Round Lake, there was John Cross Fisheries. Founded in 1945 by John Cross the elder, the fishery and the market have operated continuously in the same location and in the same building on Belvedere Road. The building is a plain, two-story white box, tucked now in what has become an upscale neighborhood. The building was built for purpose and practicality, not pretentiousness, and stepping inside the market is like stepping back in time. I think there are still things taped or stapled on the walls that date back to 1945. It's the kind of building that, no matter how hard you might try, cannot be recreated today. It's what they call patina.

John Cross, his son John Cross Jr., and grandson John "Jack" Cross III used to sail out through the Round Lake Channel into Lake Michigan to catch whitefish. These days, the Cross family no longer takes the boat out, a practice that ended some time ago, primarily due to regulatory pressures. Still, the fish, sourced from other local fishermen, is as fresh as can be, and processed and smoked on the premises. A good many area restaurants and groceries proclaim, "We Proudly Serve John Cross Whitefish."

Unlike many Great Lakes fish markets that focus mainly on whitefish, lake trout, and salmon, John Cross Fish Market sources its fish from all over the country. Do you want cod? No problem. Calamari? No problem. Lobster? No problem. Swordfish? Crab legs? Frog legs? Scallops? Gulf shrimp? No problem. Want something you don't see? Just ask.

Jack showed me his two concrete-block smokers, which he built himself some years ago, each with massive steel doors. As you would expect, the insides of the smokers are pitch black with flavorful charred smoke.

Jack uses only maple wood. "I tried cherry," he said, "but I found that it has a bitter aftertaste. Maple leaves a sweeter finish." By the way, the smoker that Jack's grandfather used is still on-site but no longer in service. Originally it was a steel paint-storage box locker used at an old Michigan lighthouse and constructed of riveted steel. Built sturdy, just like a ship. These days, it lists a little to the side, but I have a feeling it's not going anywhere. The sentimental value is just too great.

Despite the wide variety of seafood for sale, John Cross Fish Market has never lost sight of why they are there in the first place: lake whitefish. And with a friendly staff working at the front counter, it's no wonder why people flock to the market year-round to buy fresh and smoked-on-the-premises whitefish.

As I was leaving, I asked Jack if he misses going out on the big water. He smiled a kind of sad smile. "That's where I belong."

We continue our journey south on U.S. 31 toward Traverse City, but before we get there, we make a stop at Eastport, Michigan.

I think we all know of a restaurant that when we drive by, there are always cars in the parking lot, morning, noon, and night. The **Torch Lake Café** is that kind of place. I must have driven past this place dozens of times. When I finally went there, however, I didn't go because of the busy parking lot. I went for the whitefish.

The Torch Lake Café is in a remodeled old church that was built in the 1880s. Except for the bell tower, you might not realize that it was once a church, especially with the addition of a wide wraparound porch. And inside, apart from the original hardwood floors, it looks nothing like a church. Upon entering, you first see a sleek L-shaped bar with a brick wall along the back. Behind the other part of the "L" are windows that open to outdoor bar stools on the front porch. The ceilings are dark pinewood. Modern-art portraits of famous musicians hang on the walls. The Torch Lake Café has the kind of urban coolness that might seem more at home in a big city, not rural Eastport.

There were people sitting at tables both inside and out on the porch. Others were standing and chatting, as if at a cocktail party. Outside on this particular day, there was a live band playing '40s-era Big Band music, but the musical genres rotate throughout the summer. The servers were dressed all in black and were incredibly friendly. Overall, there was this supercool vibe that I was not expecting at the side of U.S. 31 at the north end of Torch Lake.

Oh, yes. The whitefish. I first ordered the Great Lakes Chowder, with Michigan-sourced lake whitefish, walleye, and salmon. The color of this chowder was not white but rather the color of a light brown roux. There was no shortage of bite-sized fish in the creamy broth, and it was really, really, delicious. It was easy to see, and taste, that this bowl of chowder was made with love. Next I ordered the Seared Whitefish Cakes, made with whitefish, sautéed mirepoix, and panko, and served with made-in-house caper tartar sauce. The golf ball-sized cakes, flattened slightly, were deep-fried to a dark golden brown with a very satisfying crunch. Inside, there was good fish flake texture but with a melt-in-your-mouth creaminess that was simply perfection in a bite. The tartar sauce had just the right amount of tang and was not overpowered by the capers. The whitefish cakes, three to an order, are listed as a "shareable" on the menu, but, alas, I didn't share mine. The chowder, the whitefish cakes, and a cold beer made for a very satisfying mid-afternoon summer meal.

We work our way to Traverse City, Michigan, and a stop at **Poppycocks** on Front Street downtown for an interesting take on Whitefish Cakes. Featured on the "Small Plates" section of the lunch and dinner menus, the cakes are panko-crusted and served on a bed of charred lemon leek aioli and topped with bacon corn jam and greens. The cakes have generous flakes of whitefish and were very satisfying.

On the lunch menu is the very popular and uniquely delicious Whitefish Po' Boy sandwich, which consists of John Cross-sourced whitefish that is battered in a spicy Cajun buttermilk, served with tomato, arugula, and a cilantro-lime remoulade, with a ciabatta baguette serving as the foundation.

And on the dinner menu, when in season, Poppycocks might offer Parmesan Whitefish, Parmesan-crusted whitefish served with roasted lemon caper aioli.

The next stop on the Whitefish Road takes us to Leland, Michigan, on the Leelanau Peninsula. In Leland, there is a little fishing village called Fishtown. And at the east end of Fishtown is **The Cove**, a multistory restaurant that sits above and below the Leland Dam and affords the best views of both Fishtown and the waterfall below. If you are in the Leelanau Peninsula, and you are craving whitefish, The Cove is the only stop you'll need to make.

The Cove perfectly fits in with the Fishtown concept. Outside, it retains the look of a fishing shanty. On the inside, the tastefully casual décor consists of vintage boat motors, antique fishing rods and reels, taxidermy on the walls, and other historical nautical memorabilia.

You can start with the Smoked Whitefish Pâté, topped with chopped smoked almonds. Entrées include Campfire Whitefish, baked in foil with roasted pepper and onions, the Almond Whitefish, also baked in foil with crushed smoked almonds and butter, Stuffed Whitefish, served pinwheeled with lobster stuffing and served with rice, and Whitefish New Orleans, lake whitefish and shrimp tossed in a creole sauce and served over linguine. The Whitefish and Chips entrée is battered and fried, with a light texture.

I personally very much enjoyed the Garlic Parmesan Whitefish, baked in foil, with garlic, spices, and encrusted in Parmesan cheese. If you were thinking gooey cheese, think again. The Parmesan cheese provided a delightful and unexpected crunch, and the mild cheese flavor enhanced, but did not detract, from the whitefish itself.

By the way, even though the Cove Seafood Chowder doesn't include whitefish (which maybe it should!), it is a great way to kick off your whitefish meal, a deliciously creamy concoction of shrimp and clams. I ordered a cup but regretted not getting a bowl.

Our final stop on the Whitefish Road is just a few steps from The Cove: **Carlson's Fishery**. Carlson's is the main reason people visit Fishtown, I believe. Yes, there are other reasons, of course, but a fishing village would not be complete without a fish market.

One enters Fishtown from the east end, with the **Leland Mercantile** market and The Cove restaurant on your left. From there you walk down a slight hill to the water, passing a variety of retail shops housed in converted fishing shanties along the way. Carlson's is at the far west end, and the delightful aroma of smoking fish pulls people in like a winch. The various shop owners love Carlson's, because tourists must pass by in order to reach olfactory heaven.

Carlson's is focused on a small range of products, and they make everything they sell. You'll find in the refrigerated cases fresh whitefish, which was likely processed that morning, as well as daily-made smoked whitefish, smoked lake trout, smoked whitefish pâté, smoked whitefish sausage, and smoked beef jerky.

I've come across so much great fresh and smoked whitefish during my long journey, not to mention the many delicious whitefish recipes enjoyed at restaurants both fine and casual. But what sets Carlson's apart is that it is a total sensory experience. It's all about the sights, the sounds, the smells and, yes, the tastes. From the refreshing dockside environment to watching fish processed just a few feet away, Carlson's was a most fitting way to conclude The Whitefish Road.

Stories from the Whitefish Road

Sunset Beach, Fish Creek, Wisc.

Door County

IF YOU'RE LOOKING TO SIMPLY ENJOY LAKE WHITEFISH, Michigan's Upper Peninsula is a great place to go, which conveniently harvests fish from Lake Superior, Lake Michigan, and Lake Huron. But if you want to experience lake whitefish in all its glory and variety, in a very concentrated geographical footprint, Door County, Wisconsin, is whitefish mecca.

The fine folks of Door County love their whitefish, as do the multitude of tourists who visit there each summer. I have to believe that nowhere on the planet is so much whitefish enjoyed by so many in so small an area. Door County is home to about thirty thousand permanent residents but warmly welcomes several million tourists every year, most of whom will eat whitefish.

Door County is simply one of the prettiest places on earth. It is a large peninsula that juts out into Lake Michigan in northeast Wisconsin, with Lake Michigan to the east and Green Bay to the west. It features both a rugged and serene coastline and is heavily wooded. The county is roughly seventy miles long north to south and only about fifteen miles wide on average east to west.

You can drive from the base of the county all the way to the top at Northport in about an hour and twenty minutes if you're in a hurry, but chances are that you'll be tempted to make many sightseeing, shopping, and dining stops along the way. The county covers about four hundred and ninety square miles in area. And because of the temperate climate and geography, Door County is a great place to grow fruit, especially cherries, and is very reminiscent of New England and every bit as charming.

Through the interior of the county, away from the shoreline, are tidy farms, orchards, and vineyards.

Even the name, Door County, has a New Englandy ring to it. Had I to guess, I would have said that the county was named after an early settler or explorer, but in reality, the name has a somewhat darker origin.

At the north tip of the county, there is a body of water between Northport and Washington Island that was a maritime shortcut between Lake Michigan and Green Bay. This once quite dangerous strait had swallowed up so many ships and sailors over the years it became known as Death's Door. Hence, Door County.

I'm sure the county tourism bureau is thankful that it is now called Door County and not Death's Door County. And I'm quite sure the tourism bureau is thankful for its whitefish. Whitefish is on so many restaurant menus that I simply couldn't eat at them all. And I couldn't visit every fishery or smoker, either.

There are five things I discovered about Door County. First, every town or village is charming, at least the ones I visited to the north. Second, it matters little where you stay, because every village is literally minutes away from another. Stay where it appeals most to your taste or budget. Third, all of the towns have a surprising amount of public beach access, so that everyone can enjoy Green Bay or Lake Michigan. Fourth, unless you plan to stay for a month or more, you have to resign yourself to the fact that there are simply too many great restaurants to go to. And fifth, we met so many genuinely nice people in Door County that it bordered on the surreal. Can everyone really be that friendly? I understand that tourism rules in Door County, so it's in everyone's best interest to "be nice," but I've been to other "tourist destinations" around the world where people take customers for granted. Not here.

By the way, I think some sort of disclaimer is needed at this point. This is not a setup by the Door County tourism bureau. I was not sponsored or compensated in any way. The reason I came to Door County is because I couldn't write a book about whitefish and NOT come to Door County. And once I experienced Door County firsthand, I was very, very pleasantly surprised. Whether you're looking to get away for a long weekend or a few weeks, Door County is a great place to visit.

And please eat the whitefish!

Charlie's Smokehouse, Gills Rock, Wisc.

Charlie's Smokehouse

AT THE VERY NORTH END OF DOOR COUNTY, Wisconsin, at a place called Gills Rock, is a place called Charlie's Smokehouse. Here, Charlie's Smokehouse has been producing some of the best smoked whitefish since 1932, when Leroy "Roy" Voight opened a smoker on the Gills Rock dock to sell smoked chubs to tourists. Roy's son, Charlie, had worked with his father since the 1950s.

When Roy passed away in 1974, Charlie and his wife, Bonnie, took over the smokehouse. Charlie and Bonnie expanded the business, smoking more kinds of fish as well as shipping fish to customers and smoking through the winter.

In the mid '80s, they realized that the business did not really have a formal name. Make no mistake, people knew about the smokehouse, and they would often say, "Go to Charlie's and pick up some fish," or, "Go to the dock and get some smoked fish from Charlie." Hence, the name Charlie's Smokehouse.

In late 1988, Charlie's Smokehouse moved off the dock to its current location just up the hill.

I went to Charlie's Smokehouse to meet with Charlie and Bonnie's son, Chris, the third generation to get involved in the business. When I entered the store, the aroma of smoked fish was intoxicating. Charlie's currently operates three smokers on-site, and they smoke whitefish, chubs, lake trout, and Atlantic salmon. "But whitefish is our top seller," said Chris.

"Smoking fish is what we do," Chris said. "In the old days, my dad and grandfather fished, but not any longer. Our focus is entirely on smoking and doing it the best we know how."

Like good barbecue, smoking fish is best done low and slow. The best way to smoke fish, Chris explained, is to start cool and slowly build the heat and smoke. "At the end, there's more heat and less smoke, which drives in the flavor and color into the fish." Indeed, the smoked whitefish at Charlie's has intense flavor and an attractive, bronze finish.

And if you happen to be downwind of Charlie's when the doors of the smokers are opened, and the smoke billows out, you are in for a treat. The aroma of smoked fish might just send you into a whitefish coma.

I asked Chris how competitive it is with so many people smoking fish in Door County. He thought for a moment and then said diplomatically, "It's all about the relationships. You have to have good relationships with everybody in the business. You just make it work."

"When did you first get involved in the smoking business?" I asked.

"Wow," Chris said. "I don't ever remember a time when I wasn't involved. My earliest memories are of the smoker, when I would tag along with my dad, but I think I was about eleven or twelve years old when I really began helping. My first job was to place the fish on the screens. I was too short, so I had to stand on a fish box to reach."

"Is there a fourth generation waiting in the wings? What does the future look like?"

"Yes, my son Nick is already working here," he answered, "and I have two more sons who help out the same way I did as a kid. When Nick was a baby, I carried him on my back as I went about smoking. Like me, I'm sure the boys have early memories of the smell of smoked fish. The smoke is in our blood."

Fresh whitefish on ice, Henriksen Fisheries, Ellison Bay, Wisc.

Henriksen Fisheries

MY FIRST CONTACT WITH HENRIKSEN FISHERIES was not what I expected. It was not on a pier at water's edge but at a farmer's market on a beautiful Door County August morning.

You see, my goal was to meet Charlie Henriksen, the founder of Henriksen Fisheries. But among the vegetable and fresh-cut flower vendors at the Jacksonport Farmer's Market was a small ten-by-ten tent with a woman selling fish from the back of a refrigerated white van. On the side of the van was a sign with a picture of a lake whitefish and the words, "Henriksen Fisheries."

Meet Kristie Moss-Henriksen, and she is selling whitefish. Or, as she often says, "slinging fish."

Before I introduced myself, I stood a few yards away and watched. The people never stopped coming! True, there were many vendors selling vegetables, and only one selling fish, but I could see that something special was going on here. One after another they came, and many of them knew Kristie by name.

"Kristie, how ARE you!"

"I'm amazing!" she said. Another woman approached, and Kristie recognized her and gave her a long hug. The woman was experiencing a hardship of some sort or another, and Kristie said, "Have some whitefish dip, on the house. Would you like cream cheese or goat cheese?"

The woman hesitated. "Here, take them both," Kristie said, "and here are some crackers." There was another hug, and as the woman was leaving, Kristie said, "I appreciate you!"

Something special was going on here. Sure, I get it. In a small community, people know each other, but there was definitely something special going on here.

Another woman approached. "I'd like some whitefish cakes," she said.

"Two or four?" Kristie asked. "Hmmm, give me four," she answered. People always ordered four, it seems.

"The fish is already cooked, so you don't need to worry about that," Kristie explained. "But you want to get them refrigerated right away. How far do you need to go?

"Not far," the woman said.

"Great," said Kristie. "I like to pan-fry mine, so you get that amazing crust on the outside."

"You're a dear!" said the woman before she turned to walk away.

Kristie is the daughter-in-law of Charlie Henriksen and the wife of Charlie's son, Will. I introduced myself. She lit up as if meeting an old friend.

I was not expecting to find someone like Kristie "slinging fish." She's a force of nature. Her smile and her positive attitude were infectious, and by the time a customer left, they were smiling and feeling like they just made a new best friend.

Kristie is "five years in," having joined the business after marrying Will.

"How did you fall in love with the fish business?" I asked.

She laughed. "Well, I was first enamored with my husband, and then I became enamored with the fish."

And Kristie has had an impact at Henriksen's, taking on the retail side of the business and expanding into prepared foods rather than just selling wholesale fresh fish. Will, the second-generation Henriksen, continues by guiding the fishing operation.

"At first, I just listened," she explained. "I listened to Will, and I especially listened to Charlie. He started it all. I'm still listening. And they've allowed me to do some things that I think have grown the business. The first thing I learned was the philosophy. We're not here simply to sell fish. We're here to feed and support our community. They depend on us for food. They depend on us to put food on their tables. Sometimes that means even donating food. But you really need to talk to Charlie," Kristie said. "He can tell you everything you need to know."

"I will," I said. "Please let him know I'm on my way."

So, as I left to catch up with Charlie, we said our goodbyes, and I felt like I just made a new best friend.

"I'm here to see Charlie," I announced to Angela, who was working behind the counter at Henriksen's Fish House, their new retail store and processing facility in Ellison Bay. But before Angela could do anything, I heard a voice.

"I've been expecting you!" the voice bellowed from a room behind the counter. Soon, Charlie Henriksen appeared in the doorway. "Did you meet up with Kristie?" he asked.

"I did."

We shook hands and Charlie invited me into the back room. He sat at a small table just inside the door. "Give me a few minutes," he said. "I need to finish this paperwork." In the middle of the room was a staffer, donned in an apron and plastic gloves, forming whitefish patties by hand on a stainless-steel table.

Charlie looks like a fisherman. By that I mean he has the handsome, rugged look of someone who spends more time on the water than on land. A whitish beard. Not a long beard, mind you, but a sailor's beard, a beard that looks like he just returned home from a few weeks at sea. And he has the voice of a fisherman, baritone, not quite raspy. If Hollywood needed someone to portray a big-water fisherman, they would pick this guy.

With most of his life spent on the water, Charlie has earned "the look."

"I'm done with my paperwork," said Charlie. "Sorry to make you wait."

Then Charlie bellowed again, "Hey, have we got an extra chair around here?" A folding chair appeared. I sat down.

Charlie is an imposing man. And the first impression is that he's a bit gruff, and I'm pretty sure he can be. But he wasn't gruff with me. In fact, I detected a certain kindness in his voice, and a great smile. "So, how did your talk with Kristie go?" he asked.

"It went well," I said. "I learned a lot and I think she's a great ambassador for you. She seems to sell a lot of fish, and she sure makes a lot of friends."

"Yes," Charlie said with another smile, as if to say, "Tell me something I don't already know."

Charlie's journey to owning a fishery is different than almost everyone else I spoke with, in the sense that he was not born into the business. He built the business. He grew up on the north side of Chicago and studied engineering in college. In 1972, while Charlie was still in college, his parents chased their dream and bought a small hotel in Ellison Bay called the Hotel Disgardin. Charlie would often spend weekends and summers helping his parents renovate the place. While doing that, neighbors and friends would ask Charlie to help them fish. Eventually, he ventured out on his own, in 1987, and bought his first boat in 1989.

These days, Charlie, Will, and a small crew often find themselves out on the water well before dawn. "It makes for a long day," he said, "but it's just what you do. I don't count hours. Never have."

"Is the fishery business in Door County competitive?" I asked.

"It's competitive in the sense that if I catch two hundred pounds of fish and the other guy catches three hundred pounds, he's happy. But if I catch two thousand pounds and he catches one thousand pounds, he's unhappy, even though one thousand pounds is a lot more than three hundred." Charlie laughed.

One thing I learned as I talked to fisheries in Wisconsin and Michigan is that these days, the commercial fishing industry tends to be more cooperative than competitive.

"The reality is that we all tend to help each other out, if need be," he continued. "Fishing fluctuates day by day, and season by season, but we all have customers we need to take care of. In the long run, it's better if we work together than trying to go it alone."

Henriksen Fisheries only fishes for whitefish. Charlie echoed what Kristie had told me earlier in the day. "We're in the business of catching and selling fish, but our responsibility is to serve the community. We're just not providing fish, we're providing food. Whitefish were born to be food. It's our job to put it on the plate."

Henriksen's, even as they branch out with retail sales, is still primarily a wholesaler. They have about thirty restaurants and smokers that depend on them to deliver fresh fish daily.

A big part of this industry cooperation is what Charlie calls "fish politics," doing the behind-the-scenes work to ensure the industry is represented and that the industry, and most importantly the fish, is sustainable. Charlie has served more than thirty years as the president of the Great Lakes Commercial Fishing Association. You would often find Charlie at regional, state, and local town hall meetings. He has served as the chair of the Lake Michigan Commercial Fishing Board and the Wisconsin Invasive Species Council.

Charlie invited me out to the processing area. The place was spotless and nearly empty. It was late morning, and the place had already been hosed down for the day. "Where are all the fish?" I asked.

"Some of it is in the freezer," he explained, "but most all of it is already on the way to our customers." This is why, in Door County, restaurants can legitimately claim that the whitefish on the dinner plate was likely swimming that morning.

We walked to the back of the building and Charlie opened the loading dock door to show me where they store equipment. "How much longer can you keep doing this?" I asked. Not a word. Charlie just looked at me and gave me that Hollywood smile.

Oilers hanging at Carlson's Fishery, Leland, Mich.

Oilers

AS I VISITED VARIOUS FISHERIES, I noticed one common thing among them: The workers were all wearing "oilers." At least that's what the old-timers call them.

An oiler is a weatherproof bib overall that fishermen wear out on the lake and fish cutters wear in the processing plants. Today, the oilers are made with a waterproof PVC coating, but back in the day, heavy canvas fabric was coated with oil to make them waterproof. Hence, the name oilers.

Commercial fishing, obviously, can be a wet and cold industry. For those out on the water, fishermen need a protective layer from the spray and the cold. In the plant, the cutters need waterproof protection from the wet fish, the ice, the scales, and the entrails, not to mention the thorough hosing down of the premises after the processing is completed for the day.

Oilers can come in a variety of colors, but gray-green, orange, and blue tend to be what I noticed most. Orange oilers tend to be worn for safety reasons when out on the lake. In the processing plant, I've seen all the colors, but white oilers, like those I saw worn by the cutters at Baileys Harbor Fish Co. in Baileys Harbor, Wisconsin, seem to lend an air of purity and cleanliness, not unlike why doctors or nurses or chefs wear white, especially when customers can watch the processing for themselves.

For fishers, the oiler is the uniform of the profession.

I'm sure that there are various companies making oilers, but from my experience, a Swedish company called Grundéns is the bib of choice in the Great Lakes region. And they're easy to spot, as the name "Grundéns" is spelled vertically on both shoulder straps of the bib.

Fish Boils at the famous White Gull Inn, Fish Creek, Wisc.

The Fish Boil

THE WORDS "FISH" AND "BOIL" ought not to reside in the same sentence. To be sure, the idea of boiled fish doesn't sound that appealing … or appetizing. Give it to me smoked, broiled, fried, grilled, or baked, but boiled? No thank you.

But there is a phenomenon, a ritual really, that happens almost daily during the summer months in Door County, Wisconsin, called the fish boil, and the result is truly delicious!

This is what constitutes a fish boil meal: lake whitefish, redskin potatoes, sometimes onions (but not always), perhaps corn on the cob (but not always), slaw or salad, and all topped off with a slice of Door County cherry pie (always), *a la mode*, of course. The fish is served with melted butter, tartar sauce, and lemon. Honestly, when it comes to comfort food, it just doesn't get much better than this.

But the other amazing thing about a Door County fish boil is the spectacle of it all. Before the fish reaches your plate, the cauldron in which it had been boiling is set afire with kerosene and the resulting fifteen-foot-high blaze of glory brings squeals, oohs, and aahs from the diners who had assembled to watch the theatrics. Do not try this at home!

Just before the meal is served, the boil master (I am not making this up!) grabs an old rusty coffee can filled with kerosene and, from a relatively safe distance, pours the kerosene on the fire, and then all hell breaks loose! You will experience blinding flames, searing heat, and the hissing of boiling water as it overflows onto the fire below, which most likely will extinguish the fire, spewing forth oily black smoke into the air. Dinner, ladies and gentlemen, is served.

I had to witness this culinary extravaganza for myself, so I visited the White Gull Inn in Fish Creek, Wisconsin, a stately place that has stood near the water's edge on the west end of Fish Creek since the turn of the last century when it was constructed by a well-to-do German immigrant. "Est. 1896," the white wooden sign proudly proclaims out front.

It is believed that fish boils were introduced to Door County in the late 1800s by Scandinavian settlers as a means to cheaply and easily feed many mouths at once, such as fishermen, lumberjacks, and farmers. As the number of sailors and woodsmen declined over the years, so did the number of fish boils. Fortunately, the art of the fish boil was passed down through the generations.

The fish boil was kept alive by church gatherings and fundraising events over the decades, again, as a way to feed many people at once. But in the late 1950s or early '60s, the humble fish boil began to be featured as a tourist attraction, first, it is believed, at a place called the Viking Grill in Ellison Bay, and soon after at the White Gull Inn. More restaurants realized the tourism potential and began offering fish boils to their dinner customers. Today, the Door County fish boil stands alongside the New England clam bake, the Louisiana crawfish boil, and the Carolina whole-hog barbecue as a true regional food experience not to be missed.

I arrived early on the day of the fish boil (reservations are highly recommended, regardless of where your fish boil takes place) to meet with the White Gull Inn boil master, a man named Neil Teskie. Neil is a kindly gentleman who seemed a bit like Kris Kringle wearing a t-shirt and a ballcap. A boil master is part chef, part storyteller, part pyrotechnic engineer, and is entrusted with keeping all the guests safe from harm.

The first thing I noticed about Neil, aside from his resemblance to a certain someone from the North Pole, were his hands. They are the hands of someone who has worked hard his whole life. In Neil's case, he labored for years as a fisherman in Green Bay, and then as a farmer.

Neil has been the boil master at the White Gull Inn for eight years. Before that, he was the boil master for a year each at the Viking Grill and the Sandpiper restaurant, both no longer in existence. At the age of 75, Neil doesn't know how much longer he can continue. "It's not getting any easier," he said with a smile.

The fish boil process begins at 4 p.m. to prepare for the first of three seatings that begin at 5 p.m. It starts with building a fire beneath a cauldron filled with water using ash wood. "I have a helper to get started, and then I take it from there," he explained.

I asked Neil if he ever gets burned, and he said, "almost every night," rubbing his forearm as if to say that the hair on his arms gets singed. "I have so many shirts at home with burn holes, I can't wear them!" he said with a laugh.

First, a very large scoop of salt goes into the water, less for seasoning and more to lower the boiling point of the water. "I use less salt for the second and third boils because the water is already salted," explained Neil.

Then, the potatoes go into a large metal basket, and the basket is submerged into the cauldron of boiling water. Neil meticulously keeps track of the timing. Next, in a separate metal basket, the chunks of fresh whitefish take the plunge into the boiling water. This is Neil's cue to become a storyteller for a few minutes.

As the fish boils, the fat rises to the top of the water. To eliminate the fat and keep it from reattaching to the fish, Neil reached for a coffee can filled with kerosene, and when the timing was just right, he proclaimed, "BOIL OVER!" and threw the kerosene at the base of the fire, which created a fiery explosion of sorts and super-heated the water so that it boiled over the edge of the cauldron, taking the fat along with it.

At this point, two young men came with a long metal pole and, after inserting the pole through the handles of the two baskets, lifted the fish and potatoes out of the water and carried the baskets into the kitchen for plating.

Neil received a well-deserved round of applause before the patrons filed inside to the dining room. Neil sat in a chair for a few minutes before his next "performance."

Inside the White Gull Inn, there was a side of coleslaw waiting at the table and a small little ceramic pitcher, maybe three inches tall, containing melted butter. When the fish and potatoes arrived, the fish had already been deboned (but please be aware that some bones may still be present).

Drizzle the drawn butter over the whitefish and the potatoes, a squeeze of lemon, some salt and pepper if you desire, and that's all it takes. It's a simple supper, but that's the beauty of it. The drawn butter makes the whitefish taste a bit like lobster, but the best thing about it is that you get to taste the whitefish in all its naked, unadulterated glory: no grilling or frying, no breading, no seasoning, no sauces. This is what whitefish is supposed to taste like.

And then, to conclude the night's festivities, a slice of Door County cherry pie with a scoop of vanilla ice cream.

A perfect way to end a perfect meal!

The daily fare at Baileys Harbor Fish Co., Baileys Harbor, Wisc.

Hickey Bros. & Baileys Harbor Fish Co.

WHEN IT COMES TO COMMERCIAL FISHING in Door County, Wisconsin, there are really just a handful of family fishing dynasties that come to mind. The Hickey family has been plying the waters around Door County since the mid-nineteenth century, when Martin Hickey began fishing for lake trout. In the late 1800s, Martin bought his first true commercial fishing vessel.

The original Hickey brothers, William and Martin Jr., took over the business from their father in the early 1900s. In the mid-1960s, William's sons, Dennis and Jeff, became fishermen themselves by purchasing the equipment and license of another local fisherman who had decided to retire.

Dennis and Jeff grew the business step-by-step, but they were still a small operation, running their retail store out of a garage located on the main highway that runs through the village of Baileys Harbor. But in 1985, they moved the retail operation to another garage on the east side of Baileys Harbor Bay that also included a small processing plant. In the 1990s, they purchased land farther out on the peninsula, established a commercial dock there, and moved the retail and processing operation just a stone's throw from the docks where it stands today.

In the year 2000, Dennis's daughter Carin and her husband, Todd Stuth, became more actively involved in the fishery. Carin and Todd not only help keep the fishing operation going, they have also expanded the retail operation by constructing a new store and processing plant on the site, as well as expanding Hickey Bros. Research, an arm of the company that undertakes fishery research projects for academic institutions and state and federal government agencies.

So, I went to visit Carin (née Hickey) Stuth at Baileys Harbor Fish Co. The first thing I noticed when I entered the store was a clean, tidy customer area lined with refrigerated cases. Beyond the cases and the counter, I could see the processing area, where about a half-dozen workers, all wearing white oilers, were processing what seemed like a zillion pounds of whitefish.

Carin was working alone behind the counter, and she was, frankly, overwhelmed with the number of customers in the store. She was both pleasant and business-like, and she efficiently took care of each customer, sincerely thanking each of them for their business.

Carin is impressive to watch. This is a person who grew up in the fishing business, and it's clear that she knows every aspect of it. It is believed that she is the only active licensed commercial woman "fisherman" in the state of Wisconsin.

I stood off to the side, trying hard not to get in the way. Just then, a man entered the store, and when it was his turn, he said, "I'd like to order twenty pounds of whitefish for Sunday. Is that possible?" This was Wednesday.

The man was worried. He was throwing a big party on Sunday, and he was afraid he had waited too long to order fish in that quantity.

"Twenty pounds is not a problem," Carin reassured him, "but we're closed on Sundays. You'll need to pick up the fish on Saturday." She asked him how he would like it, fresh, frozen, fillets, or chunks. As the customer left, Carin said, "Because you're picking it up on Saturday, just make sure to keep the fish on ice until you're ready to use it."

The customer nodded. "See you Saturday!" he said, relieved, as he left the store.

Carin looked at me. "Can I help you?" I introduced myself. "Hi," she said. "Until I get a moment, please talk with my son." She walked me back into the processing area and introduced me to her son. My first thought was that I wished I had worn rubber shoes.

Just eighteen years old at the time of this writing, Finn Stuth represents the fifth generation to work at Baileys Harbor Fish Co. He was busy processing fish when I walked over to him. That's a nice way of saying he was cutting and gutting whitefish. And for being still a teenager, Finn wielded his knife like a skilled surgeon, all the while answering my questions without skipping a beat.

He talked me through the entire fish-cleaning process. As he pointed to each step in the process, the person at that station looked up, nodded, or smiled. I noticed more processing machines here than at other fisheries I had visited. "We use machines when it makes most sense," Finn explained. "For example, we don't use a pin-boning machine because we think it can be too rough on the flesh. We still pin-bone by hand."

I asked if they smoke their own fish. "Yes," Finn said. "That's our smoker against the back wall." It's the only indoor smoker I had come across, a stainless-steel behemoth. I asked Carin later about why they use an indoor smoker, and she told me that it was more consistent, both in terms of the process and the final product. The indoor smoker uses wood pellets, rather than logs, is not subject to variances in outdoor temperatures, and is all digitally monitored from start to finish.

At one point, I noticed that Finn had discarded some whitefish eggs along with the other entrails. "Don't you want to keep those for caviar?" I asked.

"No," he explained. "The eggs aren't mature enough yet. We need to wait until fall until we can harvest the eggs for caviar."

"This seems like a lot of fish. How much is here?"

"I'm not sure," he answered, "but this was a pretty good day."

"What is a really good day?"

"Fishing has been good this year," Finn explained. "I don't know, I guess two to three thousand pounds would be a really good day." There had to be at least two thousand pounds on this day, I thought.

Carin came back to rescue me from the wet floor, which honestly wasn't that bad. I thanked Finn, and he returned to his knife-work.

The processing area at Baileys Harbor Fish Co. was pristine. Everything was white and bright with stainless steel tables and machinery. Every single cutter was wearing a white oiler. Crushed ice was everywhere. This is what customers see when they enter the store.

"Very impressive," I said. "And I'm also impressed by your son! He knows what he's talking about. You, too."

Carin smiled. "My dad's a good teacher," she said matter-of-factly. There was a break in the action, and for the moment, there were no customers in the store.

"That's a lot of fish out there," I said.

Carin gave a kind of half nod. "Yes. We don't just sell fish in Door County. We deliver whitefish to New York, Chicago, even Canada. That requires a lot of fish."

I asked Carin about the state of the industry, about supply and demand. She admitted that the supply wasn't what it used to be, but they have customers that need to be taken care of, both established wholesale customers like restaurants and walk-in customers like the man who just ordered twenty pounds of whitefish.

"It's definitely a challenge," she said, "but we haven't raised our prices in years. We want customers to have an affordable meal." It's a sentiment that I've seen at other fisheries as well. The lake whitefish is a food fish, plain and simple.

Baileys Harbor Fish Co. is more than just a company that harvests and sells fish. They are providing sustenance. And the staff are keenly aware of sustainability, which is why the governor of Wisconsin named Dennis Hickey as an advisor to the Great Lakes Fishery Commission, a U.S.-Canada organization dedicated to sustaining fish stocks, research, managing invasive species, and undertaking research.

I was thoroughly enjoying my conversation with Carin, but I didn't want to overstay my welcome. Before I left, however, Carin took me on a tour of their refrigerated and frozen cases to show me the wide range of products they offer.

I thanked Carin for her time and asked her to again thank Finn. I walked out the front door. The sun was shining, the sky was blue, I had whitefish, and I could see the sparkling waters of Baileys Harbor down the dusty road in front of me. This was a good day.

Harbor Haus

COPPER HARBOR, MICHIGAN, IN SOME WAYS feels like the end of the earth. Copper Harbor is the northernmost town of the Michigan mainland, and once you get there all you can see, all the way to the horizon, is the great inland sea, Lake Superior.

The directions to get there are easy. Take U.S. Highway 41 north up the Keweenaw Peninsula until it ends. You've arrived.

First, a little history.

Copper Harbor was officially established in 1844 with the building of Fort Wilkins, a U.S. Army outpost, to keep an eye on things. As the name obviously implies, Copper Harbor is where the copper mined from the copper-rich Keweenaw Peninsula was transported to the industrial cities along the shores of the Great Lakes. No doubt that the readily abundant and cheap lake whitefish helped feed the miners and mariners who worked there.

And while Copper Harbor has never been known as a fishing village, the residents know and love their lake whitefish. To gaze out over the water, it's not hard to imagine the millions of whitefish swimming out there in the cold, clear, deep water of Lake Superior.

Copper Harbor today is not what I would call New England-esque, but there is definitely a certain charm to it. The architecture tends to lean toward early 1950s Michigan tourist style. Log cabins. Motels. Souvenir shops. Motels *attached* to souvenir shops.

With only about two hundred year-round residents, it's hard to even call this a village. Let's call it a hamlet. And if you head east and turn north onto 1st Street (there are only ten "Streets" in the whole town, and only three blocks north to south) and take it north until you hit the shore, there is a restaurant that looks like it doesn't quite belong there: Harbor Haus.

As you might guess by the spelling, this is a German-themed restaurant. The exterior has a certain *ersatz* Bavarian look, and the menu features the obligatory *wurst, schnitzel, spätzle*, and *sauerkraut*. But don't be fooled by the Bavarian motif. This is fine dining at its best.

"This restaurant really doesn't belong here," I said to Dan Harri, the executive chef and partner at Harbor Haus.

"What do you mean?" he asked, puzzled.

"If you look at this menu," I explained, "it seems to me that it is more at home in Chicago or New York City."

Chef Dan smiled. I think that this is precisely what he wants to hear. And it makes sense. Although he was born in Copper Harbor, he earned his culinary chops working in Jamaica, the Bahamas, St. Lucia, and Miami. He has cooked for several presidents.

And to accompany such fine fare and personal service is an unmatched view of Lake Superior through large wall-to-wall windows. There's not a bad table in the place. And there's even outdoor dining when weather permits.

"I would call what we do creative American fare," he explained. "And no chicken. Zero chicken."

"What about the German dishes?"

"When we purchased the restaurant in 2015, it was primarily a German restaurant. Although we are slowly moving away from the German food, we can't move away completely because we have a lot of customers who come for it. They like it, so we keep it. And we still have an Oktoberfest celebration every year."

"Speaking of customers, where do they come from? This place is in the middle of nowhere."

"They come from literally everywhere," Chef Dan said. "Sometimes when I take a break, I'll do a PLI."

"PLI. I don't follow."

"Parking Lot Indicator," Chef Dan said with a smile. "I go outside and look at the license plates. Customers come from all over America. If they can make it to Copper Harbor, they will eat here."

"What about staffing? It must be tough finding people to work here."

"Not at all. My cooks have basically been with me since I've been here. Our servers come back year after year. If not, it's not hard to hire new staff because I believe this is the best place to work in Copper Harbor. But it's more than just the money. We're building a culture here."

At that, Chef Dan reached underneath his chef's jacket to a black t-shirt. I thought he was going to show me a tattoo. Thankfully, he didn't. But there on the sleeve of his t-shirt were the letters NDZ.

"Do you know what NDZ stands for?" he asked.

"Not a clue."

"No Drama Zone," he said. He was not smiling this time. He was serious. "Everyone in the kitchen wears this shirt. We're at the top of the food chain. By that I mean that we charge a higher price for our food and service, so it has to be perfect. It has to look perfect, and it has to taste perfect. Every plate. Every time."

He continued, "And this extends to our hosts, our servers, our bartenders. It's always done with a smile and a respect for our customers. It's always 'please and thank you.' We are polite people serving polite people."

At this point, Chef Dan surprised me. "Hey, do you want to see the kitchen?" He was like a kid wanting to show off his baseball card collection.

We walked into the kitchen. I immediately noticed how focused the staff was … how calm. Nothing was harried. No banter or chatter or joking around. No tension. Just focus.

And just as Chef Dan described, everyone in the kitchen was wearing a black t-shirt with the letters NDZ on the left sleeve. On the back of the t-shirts were the words "Harbor Haus Culinary Team." One of the cooks had a t-shirt that said, "Harbor Haus Culinary Team" with the previous year's date. This wasn't his first Harbor Haus kitchen rodeo.

Chef Dan likely gave his team a heads-up that there might be a visitor in the kitchen, but you couldn't fake this. Everyone was polite and focused. Everyone knew exactly what they were supposed to be doing. I visited Harbor Haus in early September, so this culinary team had worked together since May and, actually, for years preceding. Everything seemed intuitive, as if words weren't necessary.

Okay, it was time for *me* to get focused.

"What about the whitefish?" I asked. "Over here," he said. We walked over to the flat-top grill. "We serve several hundred pounds of whitefish every day."

The cook at the grill was working on several whitefish entrées for the evening. Every single meal at Harbor Haus is cooked to order, but in the case of the Planked-Style Whitefish, a few were already on the grill because it takes a bit longer to prepare, in part because of the bacon.

"This is our most popular dish," said Chef Dan, "so these won't stay here long. We're just getting a head start."

Chef Dan grabbed a spatula and scooped up a fillet and, cradling it like a baby, showed it to me. "Isn't this beautiful?" I didn't respond, because he already knew the answer. He gently returned the fillet to the grill, and slightly nodded to the cook, as if to say, "I'm sorry for interrupting" or "keep up the good work."

Next to that were the Griddle Seared Lake Superior Whitefish, which already had some orders for them. This entrée features a *beurre monté*, which is a kind of melted lemon butter.

"We very slowly melt solid butter and then gently infuse it with lemon." explained Chef Dan. "It takes time."

"How does all this work so well?"

"If I weren't with you now, I'd be right here on the line with this team," he said. "I lead by example. I'm a 'show and tell' kind of manager. It's hard work, but this team gets along well and it's a great environment to work in."

I sincerely thanked Chef Dan and the culinary team and left the kitchen. About an hour later, I returned to Harbor Haus with my wife for a meal. Indoors, tables were set with linen tablecloths and napkins, and substantial silverware. We opted to eat outdoors on the patio so we could enjoy the spectacular view and the fresh air.

I ordered the Tempura Whitefish appetizer, which I had been dreaming about for months, and the soup du jour, which on this night was Whitefish Corn Chowder.

The chowder came first. I could see pieces of whitefish, of course, but also bits of celery, carrots, and corn, all in a creamy broth. There was a pleasant hint of bacon, not overpowering. Chef Dan had already told me that when the *roux* is being made, he adds applewood smoked bacon. Delicious.

The Tempura Whitefish came next, and I was not disappointed. Tender whitefish fried in a crispy tempura batter and served with grated carrots, spicy soy-ginger sauce, and topped with pickled ginger and a rosemary sprig for garnish.

For the entrée, I ordered the bacon-wrapped Planked-Style Whitefish with a honey orange ginger glaze. A couple from West Virginia dining at the table next to us said that they had eaten at Harbor Haus for six consecutive nights, and the gentleman had ordered the bacon-wrapped whitefish twice.

Many people say that Harbor Haus is the best restaurant in Michigan's Upper Peninsula. I would argue that you would have a difficult time having a better dining experience anywhere on the planet.

There's no doubt that people routinely drive the forty-five miles up from the city of Houghton to Copper Harbor, or from points much farther away, to eat at Harbor Haus and to enjoy the food, the amazing view, and the whitefish. Personally, I would drive a million miles to eat there. It's that good.

Lake Medora, Copper Harbor, Mich.

Medora Whitefish

SPOILER ALERT. THIS IS A SAD STORY.

Lake Medora is a freshwater lake in Michigan's Keweenaw Peninsula, just south of Copper Harbor. It is a man-made lake, created in the 1860s when the Mosquito River was dammed to provide electric power to the Medora Copper Mine. The lake is shallow, only about thirty feet deep, and cold. Lake Medora is just shy of seven hundred acres, and the lake bottom consists of gravel, sand, and rock, a perfect environment for spawning.

The fish ecosystem once consisted of yellow perch, smallmouth bass, and lake whitefish. But there was something special about the lake whitefish then living in Lake Medora. It was a unique "strain" of lake whitefish, similar, yet different from the whitefish found in nearby Lake Superior. What made this strain unique was its ability to feed off the surface and its willingness to take a fly, like salmon or trout, making it more of a sport fish than a commercial fish. Lake whitefish traditionally feed off the bottom of the lake, not the surface.

In 1926, a biologist from Northern State Teachers College (now Northern Michigan University) by the name of John N. Lowe studied Lake Medora. After doing so, Mr. Lowe gave the following warning: Keep walleyes out of Lake Medora; do not stock the lake with them. He predicted that walleyes would outcompete whitefish for food and might not even survive themselves.

Fast forward to 1971. Due to requests from lake owners, walleyes were introduced into Lake Medora as a way to control the perch population. Professor Lowe's warning about human intervention proved to be true. By 1992, Medora whitefish were totally eliminated from Lake Medora.

VanLandschoot & Sons, Munising, Mich.

VanLandschoot & Sons

MY PHONE RANG EARLY ON A SUNDAY MORNING. "Hi. This is Dennis Van-Landschoot. We'd love to have you come visit us. Just let us know what you'd like to see."

Just a few days earlier, I had sent a message to a general email address, so I wasn't quite sure when anyone would read it, if at all.

One thing I've learned is that fishers in general are people of few words. They tend to be soft-spoken. But if there is a more optimistic guy in the city of Munising, Michigan, I'd like to meet him. Dennis is the fourth generation of brothers and cousins, nieces, and nephews, operating VanLandschoot & Sons Fishery, and is its president.

On the Friday following the Sunday morning call, Dennis was waiting in front of the retail store when I pulled up at the agreed upon ten o'clock. "There's lots to see today," he explained. "The boat came in a little while ago, and we're processing fish now."

We sat down to talk and I tried to break the ice. "How's business?"

"Business is great," he beamed.

I believed him. Dennis brings a level of enthusiasm to commercial fishing that is not only rare, it's contagious. I wanted to know more. I wanted to see more.

"Wholesale is still the biggest part of our business, and we supply a lot of restaurants, even as far away as Detroit. Retail is growing here at the fish market, where we sell fresh, smoked, and frozen fish as well as a wide variety of merchandise. And we just launched a food-truck business in Marquette as a way to reach out to new customers."

In 1906, Philip VanLandschoot immigrated from Belgium and landed in Gladstone, Michigan, which is on Little Bay de Noc on Lake Michigan, just north of Escanaba in Michigan's Upper Peninsula. He took on various odd jobs until he became a fisherman's apprentice with Schowy Brothers Fish Co. in Gladstone. It was then that he knew his future. What he could not have foreseen was the family legacy it would create.

So, in 1914, Philip VanLandschoot launched his fishing business and, for thirty years, successfully operated out of Gladstone.

Eventually joining Philip were his four sons, Paul, Joe, Jerome, and Francis, hence "VanLandschoot & Sons." In 1942, the family moved to Munising, where they built permanent piers and shanties on the west side of Munising Bay on Lake Superior.

In the mid-1960s, Paul's son Jerome, anticipating the banning of gill nets on the Great Lakes, was key in developing the trap net, an innovation that was so significant that it may have saved commercial fishing on the Great Lakes.

Dennis and I walked out to the dock, and moored there was the *Max B*, their Munising fishing boat that was built in 1957 and refurbished in 1981. From there, we walked into the fish processing room. This is where I met Paul VanLandschoot.

Paul VanLandschoot is Dennis's cousin. Paul, I would say, is the current patriarch of the VanLandschoot fishing family and is sort of a living legend, not just in Munising but in the commercial fishing industry.

"This is Paul," Dennis said.

"Hi," said Paul. "Excuse me." Paul turned around and walked away. A minute later he returned. "I washed my hands," he said. "I didn't want to shake your hand after handling fish all morning."

I laughed. "No problem," I said. Already I liked this guy. Now in his early seventies, Paul currently represents the most direct hands-on fishing legacy currently at VanLandschoot & Sons. Grandson of Philip and son of Paul Sr., Paul has spent his entire life on the water. He knew his grandfather. He fished with his father. He knows the lake. He knows lake whitefish.

He explained to me how fishing is cyclic, that it changes year to year, but it always comes around. He told me how you can determine the success or failure of a fishing season based on the amount of ice that formed on the lake the previous winter.

And he told me that whitefish are adapting to the warmer water, evolving really, becoming leaner and less oily. This comes not from a marine biologist, but from someone who has handled whitefish daily for his entire life. As I said, he knows the lake and he knows the fish.

A well-known story around these parts, even featured in the local Munising historical museum, is the time Paul was out on the water with his father, Paul

Sr., when he was a boy. It was an exhausting day on Lake Superior, and on the return trip, the young Paul asked his father if he'd like him to pilot the boat. His father told Paul to just sit back and rest, that he'd earned it. It didn't take long for the young Paul to fall asleep in the darkness, but he was jolted awake when the boat his father was piloting ran aground unexpectedly. His father had also fallen asleep!

"We had to go in reverse full speed and the noise we made woke up the whole town. Lights were turning on all over Munising," he said with a laugh.

While we talked, an old pickup truck backed up on the pier. It was a young man from another fishery. Their boat recently sank, and until they got the boat repaired, they needed some fish to take care of their customers. Paul was happy to help. After they had loaded the bins filled with fish and ice into the truck, the fellow said, "What does this come to?"

Paul said, "Oh, I don't know. You need to go into the office and settle up with Sydney." Sydney Curtis is Paul's granddaughter and the fifth generation to work at the fishery. I went to the office and retail store to meet her.

Sydney began helping around the docks when she was fourteen. Still only in her twenties at the time of this writing, Sydney is in charge of what they call "land operations." She's worked in every aspect of the business, from helping on the boat, processing fish, and retailing. Initially she wanted to venture elsewhere following college, but the call of the family fishery and the opportunities it represented drew her back to the business.

As I talked with Sydney at the retail counter, I couldn't help notice a monster stuffed whitefish hanging on the wall behind her.

Most whitefish that are harvested these days weigh about seven pounds, give or take. "This whitefish weighed twenty-six pounds," said Dennis. "Biggest one we've ever seen, so we had it mounted."

For me, that giant lake whitefish represents more than just a trophy. In a way, this regal whitefish is symbolic of the VanLandschoot family itself. Its history. And its future. Somewhere, above the misty gray sky over Lake Superior's Munising Bay, I think Philip VanLandschoot is probably smiling.

100% Great Lakes Fish Pledge

I FIRST BECAME AWARE OF THE "100% PLEDGE" from Dennis Van-Landschoot, who runs the family-owned VanLandschoot & Sons Fishery in Munising, Michigan.

The pledge is an initiative of an organization I never knew existed, the Great Lakes St. Lawrence Governors and Premiers. The organization consists of U.S. governors and Canadian premiers who lead states and provinces that border the Great Lakes, with the mission of protecting those waters from environmental impact, overfishing and invasive species.

The goal of the initiative is to show how 100 percent of commercially caught fish from the Great Lakes can be used for things other than food. The initial focus is on lake whitefish with subsequent initiatives planned for other Great Lakes fish.

"Only about half of every fish we process goes for food," explained Dennis. "That means that everything else, like the heads, bones, and skin, go to waste. Now, we have pledged to use 100 percent of the fish."

Wait. How can you possibly use the head, bones, and skin for anything but perhaps fertilizer? As it turns out, fertilizer is indeed a big use for fish by-products, but those same by-products can be used in medicines and dietary supplements, like calcium, collagen, and fish oil, as well as cosmetics.

And discarded whitefish skin can be used, believe it or not, for belts, wallets, and purses as a substitute for animal leather. Well, I didn't quite believe it, so Dennis showed me some whitefish skin wallets and other things they sell in the gift shop adjacent to their fish market.

And VanLandschoot & Sons is not alone. At the time of this writing, there are about three dozen fisheries in the U.S. and Canada that have made the "100% Pledge," including some fisheries I visited for this project: Baileys Harbor

Fish Co., Big Stone Bay Fishery, Carlson's Fishery, and Henriksen Fisheries.

I'm reminded of how years ago, New England fishermen considered sea urchins a nuisance, and they discarded them by the truckload. That is until they discovered that sea urchins are considered a delicacy at sushi restaurants around the world. Now, people pay a premium for them.

Fish "leather" is not as durable as cowhide, so it is not a direct replacement, but think of the possibilities. What about fish skin smartphone or eyeglass cases? Luggage tags or bookmarks? Journal or photo album covers?

"Sustainability," explained Dennis, "is more than just protecting the supply of fish we harvest. It also means that we use all of the fish we do catch. It's just a smarter use of resources."

Hog Island Country Store & Cottages, Naubinway, Mich.

Hog Island Country Store

ALONG U.S. ROUTE 2 IN MICHIGAN'S UPPER PENINSULA, near Naubinway, there is a big yellow sign at mile marker 287 that reads, "Hog Island Country Store SMOKED FISH." Next to the big sign is a smaller sign that reads, "Fudge SMOKED FISH Pasties." The words SMOKED FISH are the biggest words, and they are the only words in red and in uppercase.

By the way, a pasty, which rhymes with nasty, is a savory pastry filled with meat, potatoes, rutabaga, and carrots, and served with either catsup or gravy, and probably not what you were thinking it was. The pasty (remember, it rhymes with nasty, not hasty) is perhaps the only regional food as popular as whitefish in Michigan's U.P.

There are a few things to know about. First, mile markers are helpful, because there's not much happening between St. Ignace and Naubinway except forests, sand dunes, and incredible Lake Michigan vistas. If you're too busy looking at the scenery, tourist attractions come up fast, and you tend to drive past them. And if you do drive by, don't expect an easy turnaround. You may have to drive miles down the road before you can find a suitable place to pull over and go back. That also explains why signs are big and bright. The bigger and brighter, the better. Yellows and reds seem to work best.

The other thing to know is that the two words SMOKED FISH attract tourists in droves. Like bees to nectar. Perhaps the only other two words that would do better would be FREE FISH.

I saw the sign with the two big red words SMOKED FISH, but I couldn't stop in time, so I had to drive miles down the road to find a suitable place to pull over and go back. When I got there, behind the big yellow sign was the very tiny Hog Island Country Store.

On a "Cuteness Scale" of between one and ten, the Hog Island Country

Store rates a fifteen. The white clapboard-sided store, I would guess, can't be more than sixteen feet wide and perhaps only twice as deep. The owners, Tom and Sandy Jacobs, have been running the store for a few decades.

"I give my wife all the credit for the cuteness," said Tom. "Okay, *most* of the credit," he said with a sly smile. At that point, Sandy entered the room and Tom proclaimed, "Hey, you just rated a fifteen!"

The building itself began its life as a logging-camp cabin a century ago and has been moved several times before landing in its present location. In a previous life, it even served as a gas station.

Inside the store, the counters, coolers, and refrigerated cases are all vintage. "They're all older than I am," joked Tom. In addition to the aforementioned fudge, smoked whitefish, and pasties, the store purveys craft jams and syrups, wild rice ("because it sells," Tom said), some canned goods, and other staples, as well as some souvenirs, books, and local honey ("We're not talking about the girl next door!" Tom explained, tongue in cheek.). On top of that, there are vintage photographs and antiques on the walls that aren't for sale. It's definitely like stepping back in time.

And behind the country store are six small white cottages that offer an authentic vacation experience of the '40s, '50s, and '60s, all with modern conveniences and all within walking distance to a sandy Lake Michigan beach. "We have guests who visit us year after year," said Sandy. "They're like family."

Tom and Sandy bought the store and cottages on a whim, having seen a for-sale sign for the cottages as they were driving by on vacation years ago. Both were Lower Peninsula residents; Tom worked in the auto industry and Sandy was an intensive care nurse.

Over the succeeding years, they have worked tirelessly to nurse the store and cottages back to life. It has been a labor of love, they will tell you.

The country store is the crown jewel, and the best things to be found in the store, in my mind, are Sandy and Tom. Trust me, you'll enjoy the chat. Oh yes, and please buy some SMOKED FISH.

Or a pasty.

Country Smoked Fish, St. Ignace, Mich.

Country Smoked Fish

WHEN YOU ARE HEADING WEST out of St. Ignace, Michigan, on U.S. Route 2, and you're in the mood to buy some smoked whitefish, the natural inclination is to make a stop at Gustafson's in Brevort.

But before you get to Gustafson's, only about eight miles west of St. Ignace, you'll see a place on the south side of the road called Country Smoked Fish. This place is worth the stop.

Don't get me wrong, Gustafson's is iconic and smokes some darn good fish. They are known far and wide. Heck, even *The New York Times* did a story about Gustafson's some years back. But for my taste, Gustafson's seems a bit too … well … busy.

I suppose that's a good problem to have, but as good as the fish is, Gustafson's exhibits the ambience of a convenience store. Sure, the four box smokers are there at the east side of the building for all to see, but inside, you can purchase beer, wine, groceries, beef jerky, clothing, and souvenirs, all while filling your tank at one of four gas pumps out front.

Gustafson's does a great business, so much so that on the day I visited, it was actually difficult to walk around the aisles. There was a line at the checkout. If you're looking for a "one-stop shop" where you can get gas, food, souvenirs, and some great smoked whitefish, Gustafson's is your place.

But situated below the enormous billboard signs for the Mystery Spot and Deer Ranch is Country Smoked Fish. I was intrigued by the simplicity and quaintness of the place. The sign out front proudly proclaims "SMOKED FISH" in big red letters. There's even a little yellow smiley face cheese head atop the sign letting passersby know that cheese and cheese curds are also sold here.

There is nothing "cheesy" about this place, however. It's the real deal.

Pull off the road onto a gravel parking lot. You can smell the smoke as soon as you open your car door. The building features a wide wraparound porch in unpainted wood. There are two bistro tables out front for sampling your purchases. Even using the word "bistro" seems out of place here.

No, this place looks like it belongs in the Upper Peninsula backwoods. Inside, the first thing you notice is the heavenly aroma of smoked fish.

"Hello! Let me know if you need help." Meet Diane, who owns and operates Country Smoked Fish with her husband, Bob. This is not a rehearsed line. Diane really wants to help. Her friendly demeanor can't be faked.

Diane has been smoking fish since she was a kid. Country Smoked Fish went into business in 1985, and the primary focus has always been on the smoking. Smoked whitefish, trout, and beef jerky make the headlines at this place, but they also sell locally sourced honey, syrups, and jams, as well as pickles and pasties. They can smoke up to three hundred pounds of fish at a time.

I asked Diane if I could get a peek at the smoker, and she hesitated. "Well, I think it would be okay," she said. "Bob is out there now, but maybe we should ask him first."

A few minutes later, Bob came in from the smoker and we introduced ourselves. I asked Bob if I could take a look at where the fish is smoked, and Bob said, "It's okay with me, but it's up to Diane." I was surprised by how each had deferred the decision to the other. I got the sense that Diane and Bob were also a little surprised. Now that consensus had been achieved, I followed Bob out to the smokers, and he couldn't have been more gracious.

"This is the main smoker," said Bob. "I just finished putting fish on the racks." Like most smokers, maple wood is used here. "We have to keep track of everything," Bob explained. "Temperature and time."

Inside the smoker, the walls are charred black, like campfire wood, the result of years and years of smoke and fat. Temperature and time are tracked manually. Bob and Diane smoke their fish a long time, upwards of twelve hours, which gives their whitefish a definite richness of flavor.

Bob then took me to a separate smoker used for beef jerky. "I built this one," Bob said. "The firebox is actually half of an old wood stove." He explained the jerky process and said, "Store-bought jerky is not real jerky. It's too soft. Back in the day, jerky was something you could really chew on."

Bob and I returned inside, and I thanked Diane and Bob for the tour and their hospitality. Their smoked fish is truly fabulous, and they are two of the nicest people you will ever meet. As I departed, they were both out tending the smoker. It's easy to see why many locals, as well as tourists, buy smoked fish from them.

Audie's

WHEN I WAS A KID IN THE EARLY 1960s, we took a summer family vacation to see the still-new Mackinac Bridge and to visit Mackinac Island. It was a big deal. We loaded up the station wagon and we headed north. The first stop was Petoskey, where we stayed at one of the many motels that had popped up to accommodate the new, golden age of motoring. Interstate 75 was nowhere near completion, so it meant a full day on the road, and I remember all of us being very tired when we checked in and Dad parked the station wagon just outside the door of the motel room. That motel, like most of them, is now long gone.

Our next stop was Mackinaw City, where we toured Fort Michilimackinac, originally constructed by the French in the early 1700s, now a National Historic Landmark and still one of the great Michigan tourist destinations. We crossed the "Mighty Mac" bridge and stayed at another motel, now also long gone, in St. Ignace, before taking the ferry over to Mackinac Island.

Back in 1962, St. Ignace and Mackinaw City—the two towns at the north and south ends of the Mackinac Bridge—were not nearly as "built up" as they are today. One of the things I still remember, even though I was a young child at the time, was how many of the motels, restaurants, museums, and souvenir shops, either legitimately or intentionally, had a colonial/Native American theme to them. The décors leaned heavily toward log cabin or tepee motifs. Souvenirs consisted of miniature birchbark canoes, moccasins, beadwork, Davy Crocket-style hats, and frontier or fort-related items. To a six-year-old boy, this was all very exotic and cemented an image in my mind of what the Straits region was all about.

That feeling washed over me again recently when I dined at Audie's Restaurant in Mackinaw City. I came for the whitefish, but the interior is done tastefully with log cabin walls and large black and white photographs in museum-quality frames depicting the construction of the Mackinac Bridge. And on the remaining wall space are vintage items that depict the region in its heyday. Oh, and there's also plenty of taxidermy. Unless you have a severe aversion to stuffed animals, you will love this place!

The restaurant started as Downing's Cafe, owned by Neil and Jeanette Downing, and was built about the same time as the Mackinac Bridge in the mid-1950s. It was a bright, mid-century diner with red brick walls and contemporary turquoise vinyl chairs and booths. A postcard from the '50s proclaimed it as "the newest and finest in town" and boasted "good foods and excellent service in a pleasant atmosphere."

The Downings operated the restaurant until 1974 when they sold it to Edgar and Audrey (Audie) Jaggi. Edgar had been working as a chef in Harbor Springs, Michigan, and this represented the opportunity to own his own restaurant. The name remained Downing's for a few years but was soon changed to Audie's. They no longer wanted a "cafe" and "Audie's," they felt, had a certain ring to it.

At first the Jaggi family—Edgar, Audrey, and their five children—lived in the restaurant to make ends meet. There was a small room that served as a living room, and two even smaller rooms that served as bedrooms. All five siblings slept in a room that couldn't have been much bigger than ten by ten. These days Edgar and Audrey have retired, and son Nick is running the business with his wife, Katie.

Nick is an affable guy with a quick smile. "If you get in the restaurant business only to make money, then you're probably in the wrong business," Nick stated matter-of-factly. "I've never counted my hours," he said, "because I practically live here. I started here as a kid, and it seemed like I washed dishes all day long. Soon my dad put me on the line to cook, and it grew from there. Today we bake our own bread. We make our own soups. We cut our own meat. And I'm very particular about the whitefish we source. We want our customers to leave happy."

Audie's consists of three dining options. There's the "Family Room," where breakfast, lunch, and dinner are served to "explorers" of all ages. This is not your typical chain-restaurant family-dining experience, however. The woodsy, frontier décor will even make youngsters feel like they are dining in a very special place. Next is the "Chippewa Room," a fine-dining space with a supper club atmosphere, with cloth napkins and tablecloths, open for dinner only. This room features similar lodge décor to the Family Room but kicked up a notch. And then there's the "Welcome Lounge," a destination for drinks and light fare, or a place to relax with a cocktail while waiting for a table to open up in the Chippewa Room.

The current décor can be attributed to Nick, an avid sportsman and local history buff. Most of the stuffed animals and fish are his. In addition to the taxidermy, there are tribal artifacts, construction tools from the Mackinac Bridge, and antique logging equipment.

"Sometimes items get donated by friends or customers," explained Nick. "Sometimes I just find things. I once found an old bearskin coat in the trash," pointing to a fur coat hanging on the wall as decoration. "I couldn't believe my luck!"

Now, before you get the wrong idea about the taxidermy and the antiques, this is all very tastefully done. Trust me on this. Think upscale north country lodge. In an age where restaurants and dining "concepts" come and go, Audie's represents a kind of stability in Mackinaw City that brings comfort to the locals and a memorable dining experience to tourists. There are few businesses in town that are older. People come to Audie's because it is a Mackinaw City tradition. Homemade comfort food. Great atmosphere. Friendly and courteous staff. Who doesn't like that?

Oh, by the way, can you guess the very first stuffed animal put on display in the restaurant? A lake whitefish! "Once in a while," Nick said, "we get a customer who is unsure of what a whitefish is. All I have to do is point to the wall."

Carlson's Fishery, Leland, Mich.

Carlson's Fishery

I'M AT FISHTOWN, THE HISTORIC FISHING VILLAGE at water's edge in Leland, Michigan, to meet with Nels Carlson and Mike Burda, business partners at Carlson's Fishery.

I find them not in an office but sitting on some crates on the dock outside the fish processing room. It is a warm, sunny September morning. A sport fishing boat is moored where they sit, and tourists casually walk past and ask questions.

"Welcome to our office," Nels said to me with a grin. Nels is the fifth generation Carlson to run the business. In fact, he is named after his great, great grandfather, Nels Carlson, a Norwegian immigrant who founded the fishery in 1904.

Not only are Nels and Mike partners in the business, they are lifelong friends. Now in their early 40s, Nels and Mike grew up in Fishtown, and it was their childhood playground. Wearing their waterproof oilers, they remind me of a grown-up maritime version of Tom Sawyer and Huck Finn.

"My family owned a store in town, and of course, Nels's family owned Carlson's Fishery," recalled Mike. "It was a great place to grow up. Nels and I would jump from boat to boat, go fishing together, and swim in the river and Lake Michigan. It was a great childhood."

Even now, Nels and Mike will have a daily meeting out on the dock, weather permitting, to talk shop. Nels is in charge of processing and the "big picture." After all, he has a family legacy to protect. Mike oversees the day-to-day operations. Yet, both are hands-on and can be seen processing fish and tending to the smokers every day. "It's a cool place to work," said Mike.

But Nels has more than just a family legacy to protect. He is protecting the very legacy of Fishtown itself.

Fishtown is one of the last working fishing villages on the Great Lakes. Fishtown is situated at the mouth of the Leland River (originally called the Carp River) as it empties into Lake Michigan.

In the early 1900s and through most of the 20th century, Fishtown was home to a dozen or more fisheries. It was a rugged industry filled with rugged men. The banks of the Leland River were dotted with shanties, storage sheds, net repair shacks, and processing and ice houses. The river itself was filled with lake-going fishing boats. Fish were plentiful, and it was an industry that thousands of people relied upon for their livelihood.

But by the 1970s, there were just three fisheries remaining in Fishtown, and just a few years later, Carlson's would be the only fishery standing. The decline was due to invasive species in Lake Michigan and tougher government regulations that favored sport fishing over commercial fishing.

Fishtown was transforming in another way, however. At about the same time, Fishtown was drawing summer visitors attracted by those same weathered shanties, docks, and boats. Fishtown became a favorite spot for artists, photographers, and tourists.

Bill Carlson, Nels's uncle and the head of Carlson's Fishery at the time, began buying up shanties along the river and even built some new shanties in the traditional style. He was looking for answers. He was looking for ways to save the business, but perhaps even more, he was looking for ways to save Fishtown from the inevitable developers. Fishtown was in his soul.

The solution came from perhaps an unlikely source: a few citizens of the Leland community who also believed that Fishtown was in their souls and worth saving.

In 2001, Bill spearheaded the nonprofit Fishtown Preservation Society, formed with the simple mission of keeping Fishtown around for future generations and maintaining its authenticity.

The executive director of the society, Amanda Holmes, found her mission as well. Although she is technically an administrator, I found her to be more of a storyteller. "Fishtown exists today," she explained, "because of luck and circumstance and stubbornness. Fishtown exists because of the foresight and the alchemy of the community."

In 2007, the Fishtown Preservation Society purchased the weathered shanties and very well-used smokehouses from Carlson's Fishery. The society also purchased the nets and equipment, two commercial fishing vessels, the gill-netter *Janice Sue*, used primarily for chubs, and the trap-netter *Joy*, used primarily for whitefish, as well as the corresponding commercial fishing licenses.

Today, Carlson's is the "anchor" of Fishtown. Carlson's is what gives Fishtown its legitimacy as a historic fishing village. The other shanties have been transformed into gift shops, clothing shops, a cheese and sandwich shop, a candy shop, an art gallery, and a sport fishing charter company. Every shop is housed in a renovated fishing shanty.

And even though Fishtown has been "repurposed," it still retains its authenticity and charm. As Amanda Holmes said, "There is a sensory richness to the place."

She's right. People go there for the weather-worn shanties, the freshness of the lake breeze, and the sound of the waterfall just a few yards up the Leland River. They go there to walk the dock among the boats. They go there to catch the wonderful aroma of smoked fish. They go there for the memories.

So, is Fishtown a tourist attraction or a fishing village? The answer is both. Fishtown welcomes more than three hundred thousand visitors a year. Yet, the good ship *Joy* still ventures out into Lake Michigan several times a week (under the captainship of Joel Petersen out of Muskegon) and returns to Fishtown with fresh lake whitefish, which is processed and sold at Carlson's Fishery.

So, what did Carlson's get out of the deal? For starters, they can concentrate on what they excel at: processing and selling the finest fish and fish products to retail and wholesale customers. And, especially, they get to enjoy the sustainability of Fishtown as a fishing village.

Keeping Fishtown intact, after all, is precisely what Bill Carlson ultimately dreamed of.

And that's what Nels Carlson and Mike Burda want, as two grown-up Fishtown kids, who understand the importance of Carlson's to Fishtown.

I got the sense that both Nels and Mike realize how fortunate they are. And both of them are hands-on owners. They are there cleaning and filleting fish alongside the other fish cutters. They are primarily the ones who watch the smokers. They are the ones who graciously and patiently chat with tourists and customers.

"We know this is a very unique location," explained Mike. "We can't grow physically, so we have to grow through efficiencies and opportunities. For example, we will process the sport fish coming in off the charter boats. We can't expand our physical footprint, but we can expand our products and the ways in which we take care of our customers."

Carlson's already has customer service nailed. When you enter the front door and walk up to the counter, the first person you are likely to meet is Mike's wife, Cassie, who will instantly win you over with her delightful smile and personality. "How can I help you," she will say, or "Just let me know when you're ready to order."

You see, it's not really a question of *if* you will order, it's *when*. Seriously, no one goes to Carlson's to browse. They go there to buy fish. Everyone who walks through the front door is a buying customer.

Carlson's specializes in fresh and smoked whitefish, lake trout, and salmon, as well as other products like smoked whitefish *pâté* and beef jerky. And while Carlson's is a full-service processor, it is smoking, I believe, that truly sets it apart.

In addition to smoking whitefish, lake trout, and jerky, they take pride in their smoked whitefish sausage. Nels did share one secret with me: They add lake trout to the sausage mixture. "We used to make sausage with whitefish only," explained Nels, "but it was too dry and didn't have a pleasant texture. It needed more fat, so we added lake trout."

He's right, of course. I've eaten smoked whitefish sausage, too, and it can have a dry, sawdust-like texture. Carlson's whitefish sausage provides a juicy, luxurious bite and is as good as it gets, with a certain unctuousness that sets it apart.

And when it comes to smoking fish, simpler is better at Carlson's.

"Our formula is really quite simple," explained Mike. "Three things. Really fresh fish, salt, and smoke. We don't mess around with maple glazes or brown sugar. Just three things and we do it well."

After the whitefish goes into the smoker on charcoal-black metal racks and the maple wood is ignited, they let the smoke, and time, do the rest. The fish gets to a 145-degree internal temperature for at least a half hour, and the smoking process ends at around 170 degrees. Time and temperature are tracked with a digital probe to get a basic sense of doneness, and then they hand-probe the rest of the fish to make sure it's done.

And when they smoke different fish together, Nels and Mike will put whitefish and salmon on the top racks and lake trout at the lowest point. "Trout has more fat, and will drip fat as it smokes," explained Nels. "Generally, we don't want it to drip on the other fish."

And even when the temperature readings hit the mark, the fish is not done until Nels or Mike say it's done, and that requires a visual check. "The fish may be done," said Mike, "but if the color isn't right, we leave them in the smoker a while longer." When the fish get the final okay, they are a beautiful bronze color.

As our conversation was winding down, Nels said, "Let's go get the fish." As Nels and Mike opened the door to the smoker, a small crowd gathered. And when they wheeled the rack out of the smoker, there were audible "oohs and aahs" from the assembled tourists. Some began to ask questions. Some moved closer to the rack. Others took photographs.

The fish were then taken out of the smoker and the racks were rolled to a separate room with six large electric fans mounted near the ceiling and then crushed ice was shoveled on the floor beneath the racks to gently cool the fish to below 70 degrees, at which time the fish was moved to the refrigerated cases.

"We usually have people standing around as we open the smoker door and remove the fish," explained Mike. "I will often ask them if they'd like a sample, even though it's straight out of the smoker."

Why? "Once they taste it, they will make a beeline to the front counter to buy some."

Mike simply grinned.

Street drain, Ephraim, Wisc.

The Elephant in the Room

WHILE THIS BOOK IS A CELEBRATION OF LAKE WHITEFISH, we would be remiss if we didn't address the elephant in the room: Whitefish in the Great Lakes region are in serious danger of disappearing. For a book that celebrates whitefish and whitefish culture, this is indeed a very sobering way to end the book.

Whitefish are harvested in the Great Lakes at a fraction of what they once were. Whitefish have had to endure a variety of conditions that threaten their very existence. Pollution. Climate change. Invasive species. Surprisingly, overfishing is not the problem. If it were, the solution would be a relatively easy one: Tie up the boats until populations return to normal. And while overfishing isn't the reason, whitefish harvest quotas continue to get reduced as a way to help address the problem, or at least prolong what some believe will be the inevitable. Fisheries are struggling to survive. Restaurants are struggling to keep whitefish on the menu.

No, the real problem is invasive mussel species, zebra mussels, and especially quagga mussels, which are virtually sucking the life out of the lower Great Lakes. You may have noticed how crystal clear the Great Lakes water is these days. This is not a good thing. It means that the water is lacking nutrients and plankton, the things fish need to survive. Crystal clear water also means that more ultraviolet rays go deeper into the water and are more intense, often sunburning young whitefish and creating unwanted algae.

The invasive sea lamprey used to be the main problem whitefish faced, but that has been dramatically reduced through the use of "lampricide" chemicals. Now, the focus is on invasive mussel species. And the only way to truly solve the whitefish problem is to deal with the root cause: eliminating the mussels. Quagga mussels blanket the lake beds of Lake Michigan, Lake Huron, Lake

Erie, and Lake Ontario, and at the time of this writing, there is no practical, effective solution to eliminate them. Fortunately, Lake Superior has, at least for now, been largely spared of widespread mussel invasion.

There are reasons to be hopeful, however. A single large whitefish female can deposit upwards of one hundred thousand eggs per season. The fish needs to lay that many eggs because perhaps only ten thousand eggs will become larvae, and an even smaller percentage will become fish. Even if they develop into fish, not all of them will live to maturity.

It's a numbers game and the law of averages. For lake whitefish, the goal is to get as many of those one hundred thousand eggs as possible to reach maturity. That's why a single maple tree will send millions of seeds fluttering to the ground in its lifetime, because only a few seedlings will survive to reach full maturity.

The good news is that the lake whitefish now has a fighting chance. Pollution in the Great Lakes and the rivers that feed into them has been reduced dramatically. Fishermen tell me that seeing a sea lamprey is no longer a daily occurrence, and some now say they can go weeks without seeing one.

There are biologists who are now sowing whitefish eggs upstream in rivers, attempting to "train" whitefish into spawning in rivers again, something they previously did instinctively. Biologists are also experimenting with transplanting whitefish into inland lakes and ponds, where they can survive until the mussel problem can be adequately addressed.

And let's not count out the lake whitefish itself. The goal of any species, *fauna* or *flora*, is to survive and propagate. We are seeing whitefish stubbornly adapt to the bad hand they've been dealt. Whitefish in Green Bay, for example, have rediscovered rivers in which to spawn and the number of fish making it to maturity is clearly noticeable by fishermen. Whitefish, if given a chance, will likely find a way to survive.

So, that's what we must do. Give whitefish a chance.

To save something, is to want something saved.

Whitefish culture is alive and well at Manley's, St. Ignace, Mich.

Epilogue

THIS HAS BEEN A JOURNEY I'LL NEVER FORGET. I learned more about lake whitefish than I could have ever imagined. I've eaten delicious whitefish prepared in so many creative ways at restaurants both fine and casual. But this journey was more than just about the fish. It was really about the people I met along the way.

I discovered a whitefish culture. There are many, many people whose lives revolve around this noble fish. The people who harvest it and process it. The people who smoke it. The people who prepare it. The people who sell it. And, yes, the people who eat it, and will go out of their way to buy it.

So why did I write this book? It's a valid question. Almost everyone I spoke to asked me that same question.

At first, I didn't have a good answer. I mean, I knew that there was something special about whitefish, based on its popularity, its conspicuousness at roadside diners and on menus.

The word "whitefish" or the words "smoked fish" on a sign or billboard will attract people like a hummingbird to a blossom. But as my journey progressed, I began to witness this deeper whitefish culture, and I realized how iconic the lake whitefish is to people. Whitefish is what summer memories are made of.

People love their whitefish. This is why we need to make sure we enjoy our whitefish, and at the same time make sure that it is sustainable, that it will be around for many, many more generations.

The lake whitefish, once so seemingly limitless in its existence, has been dealt a bad hand over the past century or so. Agricultural and industrial pollution. Invasive species. Climate change.

It was not that long ago that the only place to see a bald eagle was in a picture book. Now, it is a common occurrence to see these majestic birds soar overhead. The American buffalo was literally a few hundred animals away from extinction, but they can now be found in plentiful, albeit managed, numbers. These animals exist because some foresighted people wanted them saved. These animals exist today because someone cared.

The supply of Great Lakes whitefish is far less than what it used to be, and it varies from year to year, but they are far from becoming extinct, as long as we care enough to keep them around. And without the demand for these fish, the motivation to save them would be far less.

As I have said many times throughout this book, to save something is to want something saved.

Over the course of this project, I especially enjoyed talking with the fishers, those who head out on the big water year after year to set nets and harvest fish. Their work is multigenerational, and I sensed the family pride in their voices when they talked about what they do. They are keenly aware of the role they play putting food on the table.

Fishermen are a rare breed, and there are only a fraction working today compared to what there used to be. Commercial fishing is hard, demanding, unpredictable work, but the sense that I got, time and time again, is that being out on the big water, and processing their catch, is what they want to do.

I enjoyed talking with the smokers, who take pride in placing fish on racks and smoking them to perfection. Although the process for all of them is remarkably similar—fish, brine, and smoke—each of them believes that their product is unique. Oh, yes. The heavenly aroma of smoked whitefish is, truly, one of the great sensory experiences of a lifetime.

I enjoyed talking to those behind the counter at fish markets, who will hold up a fresh or smoked whitefish and say, "How does this look?" and then wrap the fish in white or brown paper, write the expiration date on it with a black marker, and offer to pack it in ice for a safe journey home.

I enjoyed talking with chefs, who continually find creative ways to prepare whitefish, and the many restaurant servers, who when asked, say, "I highly recommend the whitefish."

Keeping the demand for whitefish high will ensure that all of these people will continue to do what they do.

So, enjoy a piping hot bowl of whitefish chowder on a brisk day. Eat whitefish the way you like it prepared best: fried, broiled, sautéed, blackened, baked, or grilled. Experience a fish boil. Patronize your local fish wholesaler or retailer and select some nice whitefish fillets from the refrigerated case. Enjoy whitefish at your favorite restaurant and try whitefish prepared in a new way. Or just invite some friends over, put some beer on ice, place a large platter of smoked whitefish in the center of the table and dig in!

I hope you enjoyed taking this whitefish journey with me.

Acknowledgments

THIS BOOK WOULD NOT HAVE HAPPENED without the cooperation of others. I want to sincerely thank the following individuals for helping me tell the whitefish story and, especially, for their love of lake whitefish.

Mike Burda, Carlson's Fishery
Nels Carlson, Carlson's Fishery
Bob and Diane Colegrobe, Country Smoked Fish
John "Jack" Cross III, John Cross Fisheries
Sydney Curtis, VanLandschoot & Sons
Dan Harri, Harbor Haus Restaurant
Charlie Henriksen, Henriksen Fisheries
Amanda Holmes, Fishtown Preservation Society
Tom and Sandy Jacobs, Hog Island Country Store & Cottages
Nick and Katie Jaggi, Audie's Restaurant
Jon Jarosh, Destination Door County
Kristie Moss-Henriksen, Henriksen Fisheries
Jim Ranville, Big Stone Bay Fishery
Carin Stuth, Bailey's Harbor Fish Co.
Finn Stuth, Baileys Harbor Fish Co.
Neil Teskie, White Gull Inn
Adam Thill, Thill & Sons Fish House
George Twardzik, Harbor Haus Restaurant
Dennis VanLandschoot, VanLandschoot & Sons
Paul VanLandschoot, VanLandschoot & Sons
Chris Voight, Charlie's Smokehouse

About the Author

JEFFREY K. LEESTMA is a retired communications executive and speechwriter in the automotive industry. He lives in Northern Michigan with easy access to Lake Michigan, Lake Huron, and Lake Superior, as well as the fresh whitefish those lakes provide. This is his third book.

www.ingramcontent.com/pod-product-compliance
Lightning Source LLC
Chambersburg PA
CBHW050033040726

47599CB00015B/1666